DR. JAMES C. DOBSON

Love
FOR A
LIFETIME

Building A Marriage That Will Go the Distance

Excerpts from *Straight Talk to Men and Their Wives* by Dr. James C. Dobson, copyright ©
1980 by Word Books, Waco, Texas. Used by permission.

Excerpts from *What Wives Wish Their Husbands Knew About Women* by Dr. James C. Dobson,
copyright © 1975 by Tyndale House Publishers, Inc., Wheaton, Illinois 60187. Used by
permission.

Excerpts from *Love Must Be Tough* by Dr. James C. Dobson, copyright © 1983 by Word
Books, Waco, Texas. Used by permission.

Cover design: Bruce DeRoos/Brenda Jose

LOVE FOR A LIFETIME
© 1987 by James C. Dobson
Published by Multnomah Press
Portland, Oregon 97266

Multnomah Press is a division of Multnomah School of the Bible, 8435 NE Glisan Street,
Portland, Oregon 97220

Printed in the United States of America

Library of Congress Cataloging-in-Publication Data

Dobson, James C., 1936—
    Love for a lifetime

    1. Marriage—Religious aspects—Christianity.
I. Title.
BV835.D63   1987   248.8'4   87-14117
ISBN 0-88070-174-9

87   88   89   90   91   92   —   10   9   8   7   6   5   4   3

I'm grateful to my friend and colleague
ROLF ZETTERSTEN
for his diligent service
to Focus on the Family,
and for his invaluable assistance
in the conception and creation
of this book.

You can build a stable relationship that will withstand the storms of life."

Newlywed Nonsense

ot long ago, I was spinning the channel selector on our television set and paused momentarily to watch the "All New Newlywed Game." It was a bad decision. Bob Eubanks, the leering host, posed a series of dumb questions to a lineup of flaky brides whose husbands were "sequestered backstage in a soundproof room." He challenged the women to predict their husband's responses to inquiries that went something like this:

"Where was the exact spot your husband saw you stark naked for the first time?"

"If you and your husband ever separated, which of his friends would be the first to make a pass at you?"

"How would you describe the first time you and your husband made 'whoopee' using these TV terms: First Run, Rerun, or Cancelled?"

"Where is the last place you would have, if you could have, made love?"

Without the least hesitation, the women blurted out frank answers to these and other intimate questions. At times I felt I shouldn't be watching, and indeed, past generations would have blushed and gasped at the candor. But

Eubanks was undaunted. He then asked the women to respond to this question: "What kind of insect does your husband remind you of when he's feeling romantic?" If you think the question was ridiculous, consider the answer given by one female contestant. She replied, "A bear." When her husband realized his wife couldn't tell an insect from a mammal, he pounded her frantically with his answer card. She said, "Wellll . . . I didn't know!"

A few minutes later, the men were given an opportunity to humiliate their wives. They grabbed it. Among other questions designed to produce hostility between the sexes, they were asked to complete this sentence: "You haven't seen ugly until you've seen my wife's _____." What fun to watch the brides squirm as their husbands described their anatomical deficiencies to millions of viewers! Throughout the program the men and women continued to club one another on the head with their answer cards and call each other "stupid." That did it. I couldn't watch any more.

It has been said that television programming reflects the values held widely within the society it serves. Heaven help us if that is true in this instance. The impulsive responses of the newlyweds revealed their embarrassing immaturity, selfishness, hostility, vulnerability, and sense of inadequacy. These are the prime ingredients of marital instability, and too commonly, divorce itself. An army of disillusioned ex-husbands and ex-wives can attest to that fact all too well.

For every ten marriages occurring in America today, five will end in bitter conflict and divorce. That is tragic . . . but have you ever wondered what happens to the other five? Do they sail blissfully into the sunset? Hardly! According to clinical psychologist Neil Warren, who appeared on my "Focus on the Family" radio program, all five will stay together for a lifetime, but in varying degrees of disharmony. He quoted the research of Dr. John Cuber whose findings were published in a book entitled *The Significant Americans*. Cuber learned that some couples will remain married for the benefit of the children, while others will pass the years in relative apathy. Incredibly, only one or two out of ten will achieve what might be called "intimacy" in the relationship.

By *intimacy* Dr. Warren is referring to the mystical bond of friendship, commitment, and understanding that almost defies explanation. It occurs when a man and woman, being separate and distinct individuals, are fused into a single unit which the Bible calls "one flesh." I'm convinced the human spirit craves this kind of unconditional love, and experiences something akin to "soul hunger" when it cannot be achieved. I'm also certain that most couples *expect* to find intimacy in marriage, but somehow it usually eludes them.

> "Intimacy...the mystical bond of friendship, commitment and understanding."

To those who are anticipating a wedding in the near future, and to couples experiencing their first few years as husbands and wives, let me ask you these tough questions: When the story of your family is finally written, what will the record show? Will you cultivate an intimate marriage, or will *you* journey relentlessly down the road toward divorce proceedings, with consequent property settlement, custody battles, and broken dreams? How will you beat the odds? Fortunately, you are not merely passive victims in the unfolding drama of your lives together. You *can* build a stable relationship that will withstand the storms of life. All that is required is the desire to do so . . . with a little advice and counsel.

This book was written to provide that needed guidance. It is addressed specifically to single adults, engaged couples, and to husbands and wives who have not yet celebrated their tenth anniversaries. It focuses on the principles and concepts that will help armor-plate a marriage and equip it to "go the distance." Some of the information was gleaned from husbands and wives who have enjoyed successful marriages for thirty, forty, or fifty years. They have earned the right to advise us. We will also examine the major pitfalls that undermine a relationship, and offer advice on how to avoid them. Ultimately, of course, we will rely on the principles endorsed by a creator of families Himself. That is pretty safe counsel, to be sure.

So let's get started, shall we? There is no better time than now—during the early years—to lay the proper foundation for a rock-solid marriage. To begin, I hope you will forget everything you've seen on "The Newlywed Game." Unless, perhaps, you'd like to tell us about the last time you would have, if you could have, beat your spouse on the head with a frying pan. Move over, Eubanks. I can ask dumb questions, too!

"The key to a healthy marriage is to keep your eyes wide open before you wed...and half closed thereafter."

How Not to Make the Biggest Mistake of Your Life

heard a story about a young man who fell in love with a pretty young lady. He took her home to meet his mother before asking her to marry him. But alas, his mother disliked the girl intensely and refused to give her blessings. Three times this happened with different candidates for marriage, leaving the young man exasperated. Finally in desperation he found a girl who was amazingly like his mother. They walked, talked, and even looked alike. *Surely my mother will approve of this selection,* he thought. With great anticipation he took his new friend home to be considered . . . and behold, his *father* hated her!

This young man had a problem, to be sure, but he is not the only one. Finding the right person to love for a lifetime can be one of the greatest challenges in living. By the time you locate a sane, loyal, mature, disciplined, intelligent, motivated, chaste, kind, unselfish, attractive and godly partner, you're too worn out to care. Furthermore, merely *locating* Mr. or Miss Marvelous is only half of the assignment; getting that person interested in *you* is another matter.

The difficulties of identifying and attracting the right partner are graphically illustrated by current statistics on family breakups. Last year, there were 2.4

million divorces in the United States. What a tragedy! The average duration of those ruined marriages was only seven years—and half of them disintegrated within three years after the wedding. How could this be true? Not one of those couples anticipated the conflict and pain that quickly settled in. They were shocked . . . surprised . . . dismayed. They stood at the altar and promised to be faithful forever, never dreaming they were making the greatest mistake of their lives. For years I have asked myself why this collision with reality occurs and how it can be avoided.

Part of the problem is that many couples come into marriage having had no healthy role models in their formative years. If 50 percent of the families are splitting up today, that means half of the marriageable young adults have seen only conflict and disillusionment at home. They have felt the apathy and heard the piercing silence between their parents. It's no wonder that today's newlyweds often sputter and fumble their way through early married life.

Some are choosing not to marry because of their skepticism about long-term marriage itself. Even their music reflects this vague pessimism. Consider the words of the popular song written by Carly Simon and Jacob Brackman, entitled "That's The Way I've Always Heard It Should Be." The lyrics are devastating. They say, in effect, "It is impossible to achieve intimacy in marriage, and our life together will be lonely, meaningless and sterile. But if that's what you want . . . we'll marry." Read them for yourself:

> My father sits at night with no lights on:
> His cigarette glows in the dark.

I walk by, no remark.
I tiptoe past the master bedroom where
My mother reads her magazines.
I hear her call sweet dreams.
But I forget how to dream.

But you say it's time we moved in together
And raise a family of our own, you and me.
Well, that's the way I've always heard it should be:
You want to marry, we'll marry.

My friends from college they're all married now:
They have their houses and their lawns.
They have their silent noons.
Tearful nights, angry dawns.
Their children hate them for the things they're not:
They hate themselves for what they are.
And yet they drink, they laugh.
Close the wound, hide the scar.

But you say it's time we moved in together
And raise a family of our own, you and me.
Well, that's the way I've always heard it should be:
You want to marry, we'll marry.

You say that we can keep our love alive
Babe all I know is what I see.
The couples cling and claw
And drown in love's debris.
You say we'll soar like two birds through the clouds,

But soon you'll cage me on your shelf.
I'll never learn to be just me first by myself.

Well, OK, it's time we moved in together
And raise a family of our own, you and me.
Well, that's the way I've always heard it should be:
You want to marry me, we'll marry.
We'll marry.[1]

How strongly I disagree with the message in this sad song! It's *not* true that good marriages can no longer be forged—that husbands and wives are destined to hurt and reject one another. The family was God's idea and He does not make mistakes. He observed the loneliness that plagued Adam in the Garden of Eden and said, "It is not good." That's why He gave him a woman to share his thoughts and feel his touch. Marriage is a marvelous concept when functioning as intended, but therein lies the problem. We have fallen into certain behavioral patterns that weaken the marital bond and interfere with long-term relationships.

Among these destructive customs is the tendency for young men and women to marry virtual strangers. Oh, I know a typical couple talks for countless hours during the courtship period and they believe they know each other. But a dating relationship is designed to *conceal* information, not reveal it. Each partner puts his or her best foot forward, hiding embarrassing facts, habits, flaws and temperaments. Consequently, the bride and groom enter into marriage with an array of private assumptions about how life will be lived after the wedding. Major conflict occurs a few weeks later when they discover that they differ radically on what each partner considers to be nonnegotiable issues. The stage is then set for arguments and hurt feelings that never occurred during the courtship experience.

"Merely locating Mr. or Miss Marvelous is only half the assignment."

For this reason I strongly believe in premarital counseling. Each engaged couple, even those who seem perfectly suited for one another, should participate in *at least* six to ten sessions with someone who is trained to help them prepare for marriage. The primary purpose of these encounters is to identify the assumptions each partner holds and to work through the areas of potential conflict. The following questions are a few of the issues that should be evaluated and discussed in the presence of a supportive counselor or pastor:

Where will you live after getting married?

Will the bride work? For how long?

Are children planned? How many? How soon? How far apart?

Will the wife return to work after babies arrive? How quickly?

How will the kids be disciplined? Fed? Trained?

What church will you attend?

Are there theological differences to be reckoned with?

How will your roles be different?

How will you respond to each set of in-laws?

Where will you spend Thanksgiving and Christmas holidays?

How will financial decisions be made?

Who will write the checks?

How do you feel about credit?

Will a car be bought with borrowed money? How soon? What kind?

How far do you expect to go sexually before marriage?

If the bride's friends differ from the groom's buddies, how will you relate to them? What are your greatest apprehensions about your fiancé(e)?

What expectations do you have for him/her?

The list of important questions is almost endless, and many surprises turn up as they are discussed. Some couples suddenly discover major problems that had not surfaced until then . . . and they agree to either postpone or call off the wedding. Others work through their conflicts and proceed toward marriage with increased confidence. All have benefited from the effort.

Someone has said: The key to a healthy marriage is to keep your eyes wide open before you wed and half closed thereafter. I agree.

Noted counselor and author Norman Wright is perhaps the guru of premarital counseling, having written and spoken extensively on this subject. He discussed his views during a recent interview on my radio broadcast and made several additional observations.

1. *Couples should not announce their engagement or select a wedding date until at least half of the counseling sessions are completed.* That way they can gracefully go their separate ways if unresolvable conflicts and problems emerge.

2. *Couples need to think through the implications of their decisions regarding children.* For example, when an engaged man and woman indicate they intend to have three children, each three years apart, they will not be alone at home for

twenty-six more years once the first child is born! Couples often are stunned at hearing this. They then proceed to talk about how they will nurture their relationship and keep it alive throughout the parenting years. It is a healthy interaction.

3. *Spiritual incompatibility is very common in couples today.* The man and woman may share the same belief system but one partner is often relatively immature and the other is well-seasoned. In those instances, couples should pray together silently for three to four minutes a day, and then share their prayers out loud.

After they are married, Wright recommends they ask one another each morning, "How can I pray for you today?" At the end of the day they are instructed to ask again about the issues raised in the morning and to pray about them together. That's not a bad way to handle stress in any relationship!

4. *Another frequent source of conflict is the continuation of parental dependency in one or both partners.* This problem is more likely to occur if an individual has never lived away from home. In those cases, additional measures must be taken to lessen the dependency. Living arrangements are changed so that the person cooks his/her own meals, does the laundry, and exercises independence in other ways. Parental overprotection can be a marriage killer if not recognized and handled properly.

5. *Many loving parents today are paying for premarital counseling as a gift to an engaged son or daughter.* I think this is an excellent idea—and may be the greatest contribution mothers and fathers will ever make to long-term marriage in the next generation.

In addition to premarital counseling, another wonderful way to eliminate the unpleasant surprises of early married life is a program called Engagement

Encounter. Offered by many church denominations, it is a weekend retreat during which fiancés learn to communicate and understand each other better. Having participated with Shirley in a Marriage Encounter program based on similar concepts, I can attest to its value. For us, that weekend was a highlight of our lives together. I would not take anything for the memory of that shared experience. Again, I strongly recommend Engagement Encounter to every couple planning a wedding in the future. For more information, write to:

Engagement Encounter
953 Lake Drive
St. Paul, MN 55120

Well, the point of this discussion has been to help young brides and grooms begin their marital relationships on the right foot. Premarital counseling and Engagement Encounter are two great ways to start. Without specific effort to overcome the barriers to understanding, the honeymoon can be a blind date with destiny.

There is a better way!

M ake the choice of
a marital partner carefully
and prayerfully...you're
playing for keeps."

Suddenly, Virtue Is a Necessity

n the previous chapter I wrote, "We have fallen into certain behavioral patterns that weaken the marital bond and interfere with long-term relationships." There has been no greater example of this assault on the institution of marriage than the sexual revolution that invaded our thinking in the late 1960s. And yes, I am still angry about it. Those of us who draw our values from Scripture were aghast and dismayed when a four-thousand-year-old moral code was summarily chucked in the trash. The dam which contained the great reservoir of sexual energy suddenly gave way, releasing an avalanche of promiscuity on everyone downstream. Professors and religious leaders who should have known better used their platforms to endorse premarital sex, extramarital affairs (remember *Open Marriage?*), homosexual lifestyles, and about every wretched thing that two or four or twenty people could do together.

I still have an article in my files from *TIME* magazine, dated December 13, 1971, in which four mainline churches announced their new perspective on sex outside of marriage. They concluded after careful analysis that the commandment "Thou shalt not" really meant "maybe," and that sex was intended to be enjoyed by any two lovers of either sex who could conjure up some kind of "meaningful relationship." At last, people had been "liberated" from their sexual "bondage." Millions celebrated between the sheets.

Now, twenty years later, we're reeling under an epidemic of thirty-eight sexually transmitted diseases, with devastating new microorganisms showing up every few years. Cervical cancer in young women has soared to unprecedented rates. An AIDS epidemic literally threatens the entire human family and twenty million Americans are afflicted with genital herpes. They can expect to suffer from it for the rest of their lives. Obscene publications and films have become so offensive that uninitiated viewers often become nauseated when seeing them. Millions of girls are having babies before they're out of childhood. One and a half million abortions are occurring every year in the United States alone. And *most* importantly, the family has been deeply wounded . . . and may never recover.

"The family has been deeply wounded...and may never recover."

These are the trappings of our great experiment with liberation. Even those outside the Christian faith are now agreeing that the sexual revolution was an unmitigated disaster. As it turns out, abstinence before marriage, and lifelong fidelity were pretty good ideas after all. Some sociologists are also rediscovering the benefits of sexual restraint—as though they had stumbled onto a brand new concept. Others are still unwilling to admit that there are immutable moral issues at stake here. Instead, they are searching for ways to continue our promiscuity without being hurt by it. They are recommending "safe sex" to the adventuresome in the hopes that condoms will protect us from the ravages of disease. Tragedy is inevitable. *There is no such thing as "safe sex," just as there is no safe sin!* When a person chooses to live in direct contradiction to the laws of God, there is no place to hide.

To those who propose the condom as the answer to AIDS, let me ask this important question. If you knew that the person to whom you were sexually attracted was dying of this dreaded disease, would you depend on a thin rubber sheath to protect you from its contagion? Would you exchange sweat and saliva with that infected person? I doubt it. Speaking only of the genital implications, the failure rate of condoms when used as intended, i.e., preventing pregnancy through vaginal intercourse, is around 10 percent. How much more commonly do they tear or disintegrate when homosexuals use them in the unnatural act of anal intercourse? Who knows? Of this I am certain: There are inevitable consequences to sin, and we are destined to suffer when we defy those basic commandments. The wages of sin is death . . . still! It always will be. Condoms or no condoms.

What I am recommending to my unmarried readers is this: STAY OUT OF BED UNLESS YOU GO THERE ALONE! Not only is virginity the only way to avoid disease, it is also the best foundation for a healthy marriage. That's the way the system was designed by the Creator and no one has yet devised a way to improve on His plan. We are sexual creatures, both physically and psychologically. Our very identity ("Who am I?") begins with gender assignment and the implications of masculinity versus femininity. Virtually every aspect of life is influenced by this biological foundation. Who can deny the hormonal and reproductive forces that shape the way we think and behave? Given this nature and the vast significance it carries, even an atheist should have recognized the dangers of the sexual revolution and the changes it portended. Any upheaval of such proportions was certain to have far-reaching consequences for the stability of the family. How could we have *expected* to preserve symbiotic relationships between men and women when the rules governing our sexual behavior turned upside down? Family disintegration was inevitable.

Let me explain why sexual abstinence is so important to marriage and how it is related to the process of bonding. To do so, I will quote from my earlier book, *Love Must Be Tough*, in which I discussed the research findings of Dr. Desmond Morris. These insights were conveyed to me through the writings of my good friend, Dr. Donald Joy, and I am grateful to him for bringing them to my attention. I consider the concept of marital bonding to be one of the most vital understandings ever offered on the subject of long-term marriage. Read carefully, please.

Bonding refers to the emotional covenant that links a man and woman together for life and makes them intensely valuable to one another. It is the specialness that sets those two lovers apart from every other person on the face of the earth. It is God's gift of companionship to those who have experienced it.

But how does this bonding occur and why is it missing in so many relationships? According to Drs. Joy and Morris, bonding is most likely to develop among those who have moved systematically and slowly through twelve steps during their courtship and early marriage. These stages, described below, represent a progression of physical intimacy from which a permanent commitment often evolves.

1. *Eye to body.* A glance reveals much about a person—sex, size, shape, age, personality and status. The importance people place on these criteria determines whether or not they will be attracted to each other.

2. *Eye to eye.* When the man and woman who are strangers to each other exchange glances, their most natural reaction is to look away, usually with embarrassment. If their eyes meet again, they may smile, which signals that they might like to become better acquainted.

3. *Voice to voice.* Their initial conversations are trivial and include questions like "What is your name?" or "What do you do for a living?" During this long stage the two people learn much about each other's opinions, pastimes, activities, habits, hobbies, likes and dislikes. If they're compatible, they become friends.

4. *Hand to hand.* The first instance of physical contact between the couple is usually a nonromantic occasion such as when the man helps the woman descend a high step or aids her across an obstacle. At this point either of the individuals can withdraw from the relationship without rejecting the other. However, if continued, hand-to-hand contact will eventually become an evidence of the couple's romantic attachment to each other.

5. *Hand to shoulder.* This affectionate embrace is still noncommittal. It is a "buddy" type position in which the man and woman are side by side. They are more concerned with the world in front of them than they are with each other. The hand-to-shoulder contact reveals a relationship that is more than a close friendship, but probably not real love.

6. *Hand to waist.* Because this is something two people of the same sex would not ordinarily do, it is clearly romantic. They are close enough to be sharing secrets or intimate language with each other. Yet, as they walk side by side with hand to waist, they are still facing forward.

7. *Face to face.* This level of contact involves gazing into one another's eyes, hugging and kissing. If none of the previous steps were skipped, the man

and woman will have developed a special code from experience that enables them to engage in deep communication with very few words. At this point, sexual desire becomes an important factor in the relationship.

8. *Hand to head.* This is an extension of the previous stage. The man and woman tend to cradle or stroke each other's head while kissing or talking. Rarely do individuals in our culture touch the head of another person unless they are either romantically involved or are family members. It is a designation of emotional closeness.

9-12. The final steps. The last four levels of involvement are distinctly sexual and private. They are (9) *hand to body,* (10) *mouth to breast,* (11) *touching below the waist,* and (12) *intercourse.* Obviously, the final acts of physical contact should be reserved for the marital relationship, since they are progressively sexual and intensely personal.

What Joy and Morris are saying is that intimacy must proceed slowly if a male-female relationship is to achieve its full potential. When two people love each other deeply and are committed for life, they have usually developed a great volume of understandings between them that would be considered insignificant to anyone else. They share countless private memories unknown to the rest of the world. That is in large measure where their sense of specialness to one another originates. Furthermore, the critical factor is that they have taken these steps in *sequence.* When later stages are reached prematurely, such as when couples kiss passionately on the first date or have sexual intercourse before marriage, something precious is lost from the relationship. Instead, their courtship should be nurtured through leisurely walks and talks and "lovers' secrets" that lay the foundation for mutual intimacy. Now we can see how the present environment of sexual permissiveness and lust serves to weaken the institution of marriage and undermine the stability of the family.

Before we tuck away this understanding of bonded commitments, let me emphasize that this concept applies not only to courtship experiences. The most successful marriages are those wherein husbands and wives journey through the twelve steps regularly in their daily lives. Touching and talking and holding hands and gazing into one another's eyes and building memories are as important to partners in their mid-life years as rambunctious twenty year olds. Indeed, the best way to invigorate a tired sex life is to walk through the twelve steps of courtship regularly and with gusto! Conversely, when sexual intercourse is experienced without the stages of intimacy that should have preceded it in prior days, the woman is likely to feel "used and abused."[2] To those who are already married and now regret that the stages of bonding were taken out of order or that important steps were skipped altogether, it is not too late to work your way through them anew. I know of no better way to draw close to the person you love.

> *"Intimacy must proceed slowly if a relationship is to achieve its full potential."*

By way of summary, we can draw seven recommendations from this discussion that will contribute to life-long marriage. They are:

1. *Don't rush the courtship period when you feel you have found the "one and only."* Frank Sinatra said it musically, "Take it nice and easy, making all the stops along the way." At *least* a year is needed to allow the bonding process to occur—and even longer in some cases.

2. *Make the final choice of a marital partner very carefully and prayerfully . . . never impulsively or recklessly.* You are playing for keeps now. Bring to bear every ounce of intelligence and discretion available to you, and then yield the ultimate decision to the will of the Lord. He will guide you if you don't run ahead of Him.

3. *Proceed through the first nine stages of intimacy one at a time and in the order indicated.*

4. *Do not progress to stages 10-12 before marriage: Enter the marriage bed as a virgin.* If it's too late to preserve your virginity, initiate a policy of abstinence today . . . and don't waver from it until you are wed.

5. *Seek to marry a virgin.* This mutual purity gives special meaning to sex in marriage. No other human being has invaded the secret world that the two of you share, because you reserved yourselves exclusively for one another's pleasure and love. By following this Biblical plan, you also protect the reproduction system from new viruses, bacteria and fungi transmitted during casual intercourse. It is now known that when you sleep with a promiscuous partner, you are having sex with every person that individual has slept with in the past ten years! Virginity before marriage is by far the healthiest approach.

6. *Remain faithful to your marriage partner for life.* No exceptions!

7. *Continue to meander through the stages of bonding throughout your married life, enjoying the wonder of intimate love.*

I can hear our antagonists shouting "That's ridiculous; it's not realistic in today's world." Perhaps so, but some will hear. Some will understand. Some will survive. And as the AIDS epidemic continues to kill our friends and associates, this advice will make more sense with every passing year. And why not? It was God's idea in the first place.

Now more than ever, virtue is a necessity.

*I*f a woman feels close to her husband, loved by him, protected by him, then she is more likely to desire him physically."

Vive la Différence

y wife Shirley and I have been blessed with a wonderful relationship. She is literally my best friend, and I would rather spend an evening with her than anyone on earth. But we are also unique individuals and have struggled at times with our differences. Our most serious conflict has raged now for twenty-seven years with no solution in sight. The problem is that we operate on entirely different internal heating mechanisms. I am very hot-blooded and prefer a Siberian climate if given a choice. Shirley has ice in her veins and even shivers in the California sunshine. She has concluded that if we can have only one flesh between us, she's going to make it sweat! She will slip over to the thermostat at home and spin the dial to at least eighty-five degrees. All the bacteria in the house jump for joy and begin reproducing like crazy. In a few minutes I am starting to glow and begin throwing open doors and windows to get relief. That ridiculous tug-of-war has been going on since our honeymoon and will continue till death do us part. In fact, there have been a few times when I thought death would surely part us over this difficulty.

What is interesting to me is how many other husbands and wives struggle with this problem. It also plagues bosses and their secretaries who fight over the office thermostat. Obviously, temperature is a common pressure point between men and women. Why? Because women typically operate at a lower rate of metabolism than men. It is only one of the countless physiological and emotional differences between the sexes. It is important to understand some of the other ways men and women are unique if we hope to live together in harmony. Genesis tells us that the Creator made *two* sexes, not one, and that He designed each gender for a specific purpose. Take a good look at male and female anatomy and it becomes obvious that we were crafted to "fit" together. This is not only true in a sexual context but psychologically as well. Eve, being suited to his particular needs, was given to Adam as an "help-meet." How unfortunate has been the recent effort to deny this uniqueness and homogenate the human family! It simply won't square with the facts.

"It is a wise and dedicated husband who desires to understand his wife's psychological needs, and then sets out to meet them."

Let's look, then, at some of the ways masculinity differs from femininity. Even by this cursory examination, perhaps we can obtain a greater appreciation for the unique and wonderful way we are made. The late Dr. Paul Popenoe, founder of the American Institute for Family Relations in Los Angeles, wrote a brief article on the physiological differences between the sexes. Perhaps it would be helpful to quote from that article, entitled "Are Women Really Different?"

One of the least acceptable parts of the Women's Lib and related movements is the attempt to minify the differences between the sexes. The main thrust of their debate, or more correctly their assertions, is that such differences as exist are merely the result of differences in education and training, and therefore not basic. Since many of these differences, even if associated with education and training, have been maintained for a million years or more, it would indeed be surprising if they are not by this time deeply ingrained. But in fact, the sexes differ so markedly in ways that are not subject to change—anatomy and physiology—that it is a serious mistake to ignore them or try to make them disappear by talking.

Take a conspicuous difference, which is certainly not produced by education or training—the feminine function of menstruation. David Levy found that the depth and intensity of a woman's maternal instinct, her motherly feeling, is associated with the duration of her menstrual period and the amount of the flow. The extensive changes in the activity of her glands of internal secretion also produce marked differences in her behavior. In any large group of women of child-bearing age, 18% will be menstruating at any one time. Against this percentage, autopsies of women suicides find that 40%, 50%, even 60% were menstruating at the time they took their own lives.

Dr. Katherine Dalton, in *The Premenstrual Syndrome* summarizes many studies of behavior change that show a large portion of women's crimes (63% in an English study, 84% in a French) are not distributed evenly over time, but clustered in the premenstrual period along with suicides, accidents, a decline in the quality of school work, decline in intelligence test scores, visual acuity, and response speed. In the United States, she calculated that absenteeism related to menstruation costs about five billion dollars a year, but accidents, absenteeism, and domestic quarrels are only part of the social repercussions of symptoms that affect everyone. A book might be filled with discussion of other biological differences between the sexes, that are of great importance in one way or another, in everyday life, and are certainly not the outcome of differences in education, training, and social attitudes toward the two sexes.

Here is a quick rundown of a few:

1. Men and women differ in every cell of their bodies. This difference in the chromosome combination is the basic cause of development into maleness or femaleness as the case may be.

2. Woman has greater constitutional vitality, perhaps because of this chromosome difference. Normally, she outlives man by three or four years, in the U.S.

3. The sexes differ in their basal metabolism—that of woman being normally lower than that of man.

4. They differ in skeletal structure, woman having a shorter head, broader face, chin less protruding, shorter legs, and longer trunk. The first finger of a woman's hand is usually longer than the third; with men the reverse is true. Boys' teeth last longer than do those of girls.

5. Woman has a larger stomach, kidneys, liver, and appendix, and smaller lungs.

6. In functions, woman has several very important ones totally lacking in man—menstruation, pregnancy, lactation. All of these influence behavior and feelings. She has more different hormones than does man. The same gland behaves differently in the two sexes—thus woman's thyroid is larger and more active; it enlarges during pregnancy but also during menstruation; it makes her more prone to goiter, provides resistance to cold, is associated with the smooth skin, relatively hairless body, and thin layer of subcutaneous fat which are important elements in the concept of personal beauty. It also contributes to emotional instability— she laughs and cries more easily.

7. Woman's blood contains more water (20% fewer red cells). Since these supply oxygen to the body cells, she tires more easily, is more prone to faint. Her constitutional viability is therefore strictly a long-range matter. When the working day in British factories, under wartime conditions, was increased from 10 to 12 hours, accidents of women increased 150%, of men, not at all.

8. In brute strength, men are 50% above women.

9. Woman's heart beats more rapidly (80, vs. 72 for men); blood pressure (10 points lower than man) varies from minute to minute; but she has much less tendency to high blood pressure—at least until after the menopause.

10. Her vital capacity or breathing power is lower in the 7:10 ratio.

11. She stands high temperature better than does man; metabolism slows down less.[3]

"Men and women differ in every cell of their bodies."

In addition to these physiological differences, the sexes are blessed with a vast array of unique emotional characteristics. It is a wise and dedicated husband who desires to understand his wife's psychological needs and then sets out to meet them. That is, in fact, the theme of my book, *What Wives Wish Their Husbands Knew About Women*. Without intending to be self-serving, I recommend that young husbands read that book if they want to comprehend how their wives are unique and how their particular needs are related to happiness or depression in marriage.

Briefly stated, love is linked to self-esteem in women. For a man, romantic experiences with his wife are warm and enjoyable and memorable—but not necessary. For a woman, they are her lifeblood. Her confidence, her sexual response and her zest for living are often directly related to those tender moments when she feels deeply loved and appreciated by her man. That is why flowers and candy and cards are more meaningful to her than to him. This is why she is continually trying to pull him out of the television set or the newspaper, and not vice versa. This is why the anniversary is critically important to her and why she *never* forgets it. That is why *he* had better not forget it! This need for romantic love is not some quirk or peculiarity of his wife, as some may think. This is the way women are made, and if a particular male reader is confused about what I'm describing he should run, not walk, to the nearest bookstore or library. He needs *What Wives Wish* . . . Two million copies have sold. Of that number, 1,999,999 were purchased by women to leave on their husband's pillows at night. The remaining book went to a mild-mannered man whose wife *told* him to buy it.

Men also need to understand that women tend to care more than they about the home and everything in it. Whether your wife or fiancée has a nest-building instinct or not I don't know, but for years I have observed this feminine interest in the details of the family dwelling. Admittedly, not every woman keeps a neat house. I know some messy ladies whose mothers must have been frightened by garbage trucks when they were pregnant. But even in those cases, there is often a female concern for the house and what is in it. Husbands sometimes fail to comprehend the significance of this inclination.

Shirley and I recognized that we had differing perspectives a few years ago when we purchased a gas barbecue unit for use in our backyard. We hired a plumber to install the device and left for the day. When we returned, we both observed that the barbecue was mounted about eight inches too high. Shirley and I stood looking at the appliance and our reactions were quite different.

I said, "Yes, it's true. The plumber made a mistake. The barbecue unit is a bit too high. By the way, what's for dinner tonight?"

Shirley reacted more emphatically. She said, "I don't think I can *stand* that thing sticking up in the air like that!"

I could have lived the rest of my life without ever thinking of the barbecue mounting again, but to Shirley it was a big deal. Why? Because we see the home differently. So we called the plumber and had him lower the unit about eight inches. I recommend not only that husbands try to accommodate their wives on matters like this which concern them, but that wives tune in to their husbands' quirks and interests, too.

"How boring it would have been for the Creator to put Adam to sleep and then fashion yet another man from his rib."

One masculine need comes to mind which wives should not fail to heed. It reflects what men want most in their homes. A survey was taken a few years ago to determine what men care about most and what they hope their wives will understand. The results were surprising. Men did not long for expensive furniture, well-equipped garages or a private study in which to work. What they wanted most was *tranquility* at home. Competition is so fierce in the workplace today and the stresses of pleasing a boss and surviving professionally are so severe, that the home needs to be a haven to which a man can return. It is a smart woman who tries to make her home what her husband needs it to be.

Of course, many women are also working today, and their husbands are not the only ones in need of tranquility. This is a major problem in two-career families. It is even more difficult in the single parent situation. I know no simple solution to those stress points, although I'm convinced that emotional instability and even physical illness can occur in the absence of a "safe place." Creating an environment at home to meet that need should be given priority, regardless of the family structure.

Well, so much for this short discourse on sexual distinctiveness. Not only have I attempted to say that males and females are different . . . which any bloke can see . . . but also that God authored those differences and we should appreciate them. It is our uniqueness that gives freshness and vitality to a relationship. How boring it would be if the sexes were identical, as the radical feminists have tried to tell us! How redundant it would have been for the Creator to put Adam to sleep and then fashion yet another man from his rib! No, He brought forth a *woman* and gave her to Adam. He put greater toughness and aggressiveness in the man and more softness and nurturance in the woman—and suited them to one another's needs. And in their relationship He symbolized the mystical bond between the believer and Christ, Himself. What an incredible concept!

I say to you as husbands and wives, celebrate your uniqueness and learn to compromise when male and female individuality collides. Or as an unnamed Frenchman once said, "Vive la différence!" He must have been a happily married man.

*I*n this day of disintegrating families on every side, we dare not try to make it on our own."

Fundamentals of a Christian Marriage

n an effort to draw on the experiences of those who have lived together successfully as husbands and wives, we asked married couples to participate in an informal study. More than six hundred people agreed to speak candidly to the younger generation about the concepts and methods that have worked in their homes. They each wrote comments and recommendations which were carefully analyzed and compared. The advice they offered is not new, but it certainly represents a great place to begin. In attempting to learn any task, one should start with the *fundamentals*—those initial steps from which everything else will later develop. In this spirit, our panel of six hundred offered three tried and tested, back-to-basics recommendations with which no committed Christian would likely disagree.

1. A Christ-Centered Home

The panel first suggested that newlyweds should establish and maintain a *Christ-centered home.* Everything rests on that foundation. If a young husband and wife are deeply committed to Jesus Christ, they enjoy enormous advantages over the family with no spiritual dimension.

A meaningful prayer life is essential in maintaining a Christ-centered home. Of course, some people use prayer the way they follow their horoscopes, attempting to manipulate an unidentified "higher power" around them. One of my friends teasingly admits that he utters a prayer each morning on the way to work when he passes the donut shop. He knows it is unhealthy to eat the greasy pastries, but he loves them dearly. Therefore, he asks the Lord for permission to indulge himself each day.

He'll say, "If it is your will that I have a donut this morning, let there be a parking space available somewhere as I circle the block." If no spot can be found for his car, he circles the block and prays again.

> *"A young husband and wife deeply committed to Jesus Christ enjoy enormous advantages over the family with no spiritual dimension."*

Shirley and I have taken our prayer life a bit more seriously. In fact, this communication between man and God has been *the* stabilizing factor throughout our twenty-seven years of married life. In good times, in hard times, in moments of anxiety and in periods of praise, we have shared this wonderful privilege of talking directly to our Heavenly Father. What a concept. No appointment is needed to enter into His presence. We don't have to go through His subordinates or bribe His secretaries. He is simply there, whenever we bow before Him. Some of the highlights of my life have occurred in these quiet sessions with the Lord.

I'll never forget the time a few years ago when our daughter had just learned to drive. Danae had been enrolled in Kamakazi Driving School and the moment finally arrived for her to take her first solo flight in the family car. Believe me, my anxiety level was climbing off the chart that day. Someday you will know how terrifying it is to hand the car keys to a sixteen-year-old kid who doesn't know what she doesn't know about driving. Shirley and I stood quaking in the front yard as Danae drove out of sight. We then turned to go back into the house and I said, "Well Babe, the Lord giveth and the Lord taketh away." Fortunately, Danae made it home safely in a few minutes and brought the car to a careful and controlled stop. That is the sweetest sound in the world to an anxious parent!

It was during this era that Shirley and I covenanted between us to pray for our son and daughter at the close of every day. Not only were we concerned about the risk of an automobile accident, but we were also aware of so many other dangers that lurk out there in a city like Los Angeles. Our part of the world is known for its weirdos, kooks, nuts, ding-a-lings, and fruitcakes. That's one reason we found ourselves on our knees each evening, asking for divine protection for the teenagers whom we love so much.

One night we were particularly tired and collapsed into bed without our benedictory prayer. We were almost asleep before Shirley's voice pierced the night. "Jim," she said. "We haven't prayed for our kids yet today. Don't you think we should talk to the Lord?"

I admit it was very difficult for me to pull my 6'2" frame out of the warm bed that night. Nevertheless, we got on our knees and offered a prayer for our children's safety, placing them in the hands of the Father once more.

Later we learned that Danae and a girl friend had gone to a fast-food establishment and bought hamburgers and cokes. They drove up the road a few miles and were sitting in the car eating the meal when a city policeman drove by, shining his spotlight in all directions. He was obviously looking for someone, but gradually went past.

In a few minutes, Danae and her friend heard a "clunk" from under the car. They looked at one another nervously and felt another sharp bump. Before they could leave, a man crawled out from under the car and emerged on the passenger side. He was very hairy and looked like he had been on the street for weeks. He also wore strange-looking "John Lennon" glasses down on his nose. The man immediately came over to the door and attempted to open it. Thank God, it was locked. Danae quickly started the car and drove off . . . no doubt at record speed.

Later, when we checked the timing of this incident, we realized that Shirley and I had been on our knees at the precise moment of danger. Our prayers were answered. Our daughter and her friend were safe!

It is impossible for me to overstate the need for prayer in the fabric of family life. Not simply as a shield against danger, of course. A personal relationship with Jesus Christ is the cornerstone of marriage, giving meaning and purpose to every dimension of living. Being able to bow in prayer as the day begins or ends gives expression to the frustrations and concerns that might not otherwise be ventilated. On the other end of that prayer line is a loving heavenly Father who has promised to hear and answer our petitions. In this day of disintegrating families on every side, we dare not try to make it on our own.

Those who have not found a common faith are often left in a vulnerable position. One such lady wrote the following letter to me after her husband had left her:

Dear Dr. Dobson:

My husband recently left me after fifteen years of marriage. We had a great physical, emotional, and intellectual relationship. But something was missing . . . we had no spiritual bond between us.

Please tell young couples that there will always be a void in their lives together without Christ. A good marriage must have its foundation in Him in order to experience lasting love, peace, and joy.

Since my husband walked out on me, I have tried to rebuild my relationship with God. I am now growing steadily in my walk with the Lord, but I am alone.

Sincerely,

There is a great truth in this sad letter. The couple who depends on Scripture for solutions to the stresses of living has a distinct advantage over the family with no faith. The Bible they love is the world's most incredible text. It was written by thirty-nine authors who spoke three separate languages and lived in a time frame spanning fifteen hundred years. How miraculous is the work of those inspired writers! If two or three individuals today were to witness a bank robbery, they would probably give conflicting accounts of the incident. Human perception is simply that flawed. Yet those thirty-nine contributors to Scripture, most of whom never even met each other, prepared sixty-six separate books that fit together with perfect continuity and symmetry.

The entire Old Testament makes a single statement, "Jesus is coming," and the New Testament declares, "Jesus is here!"

"It is impossible for me to overstate the need for prayer in the fabric of family life."

By reading these holy Scriptures, we are given a "window" into the mind of the Father. What an incredible resource! The Creator who began with nothingness and made beautiful mountains and streams and clouds and cuddly little babies has elected to give us the inside story of the family. Marriage and parenthood were *His* ideas, and He tells us in His word how to live together in peace and harmony. Everything from handling money to sexual attitudes is discussed in Scripture, with each prescription bearing the personal endorsement of the King of the Universe. Why would anyone disregard this ultimate resource?

Finally, the Christian way of life lends stability to marriage because its principles and values naturally produce harmony. When put into action, Christian teaching emphasizes giving to others, self-discipline, obedience to divine commandments, conformity to the laws of man, and love and fidelity between a husband and wife. It is a shield against addictions to alcohol, pornography, gambling, materialism, and other behaviors which could be damaging to the relationship. Is it any wonder that a Christ-centered relationship is the ground floor of a marriage?

Aleksandr Solzhenitsyn, that great Soviet dissident once wrote, "If I were called upon to identify briefly the principal trait of the entire twentieth century, here too I would be unable to find anything more precise and pithy than to repeat once again: Men have forgotten God."

Don't let this happen in your home. You probably knelt together and shared a prayer during your wedding ceremony. Return to that source daily for strength and stability.

2. Committed Love

The second suggestion made by our panel of six hundred "experts" represented yet another back-to-basics concept. It focused on committed love that is braced against the inevitable storms of life. There are very few certainties that touch us all in this mortal existence, but one of the absolutes is that we will experience hardship and stress at some point. Nobody remains unscathed. Life will test each of us severely, if not during younger days, then through the events surrounding our final days. Jesus spoke of this inevitability when He said to His disciples, "In this world ye shall have tribulation, but be of good cheer I have overcome the world" (John 16:33).

Dr. Richard Selzer is a surgeon who has written two outstanding books about his beloved patients, *Mortal Lessons* and *Letters To A Young Doctor*. In the first of these texts he describes the experience of "horror" which invades one's life sooner or later. When we're young, he says, we seem to be shielded from it the way the body is protected against bacterial infection. Microscopic organisms are all around us, yet our bodies' defenses effectually hold them at bay . . . at least for a season. Likewise, we walk in and through a world of horror each day as though surrounded by an impenetrable membrane of protection. We may even be unaware that distressing possibilities exist during the period of youthful good health. But then one day the membrane tears without warning, and horror seeps into our lives. Until that moment occurs, it was always someone else's misfortune . . . another man's tragedy . . . and not our own. The tearing of the membrane can be devastating, especially for those who do not know the "good cheer" that Jesus gives in times of tribulation.

"Set your jaw and clench your fists. Nothing short of death must ever be permitted to come between the two of you. Nothing!"

Having served on a large medical school faculty for fourteen years, I have watched husbands and wives in the hours when horror began to penetrate the protective membrane. All too commonly, their marital relationships were shattered by the new stresses that invaded their lives. Parents who produced a mentally retarded child, for example, often blamed one another for the tragedy that confronted them. Instead of clinging to each other in love and reassurance, they added to their sorrows by attacking their partners. I do not condemn them for this human failing, but I do pity them for it. A basic ingredient was missing in their relationship which remained unrecognized until the membrane tore. That essential component is called . . . *commitment.*

I heard the late Dr. Francis Schaeffer speak to this issue about ten years ago. He described the bridges that were built in Europe by the Romans in the first and second centuries A.D. They are still standing today, despite the unreinforced brick and mortar with which they were made. Why haven't they collapsed in this modern era of heavy trucks and equipment? They remain intact because they are used for nothing but foot traffic. If an eighteen-wheel semi were driven across the historic structures, they would crumble in a great cloud of dust and debris.

Marriages that lack an iron-willed determination to hang together at all costs are like the fragile Roman bridges. They appear to be secure and may indeed remain upright . . . until they are put under heavy pressure. That's when the seams split and the foundation crumbles. It appears to me that the majority of young couples today, like some of those competing on "The Newylwed Game," are in that incredibly vulnerable position. Their relationships are constructed of unreinforced mud which will not withstand the weighty trials lying ahead. The determination to survive together is simply not there.

In stressing the importance of committed love, however, the panel of six hundred was referring not only to the great tragedies of life but also to the daily frustrations that wear and tear on a relationship. These minor irritants, when accumulated over time, may even be more threatening to a marriage than the catastrophic events that crash into our lives. And yes, Virginia, there are times in every good marriage when a husband and wife don't like each other very much. There are occasions when they feel as though they will never love their partners again. Emotions are like that. They flatten out occasionally like an automobile tire with a nail in the tread. Riding on the rim is a pretty bumpy experience for everyone on board.

I attended the fiftieth wedding anniversary for two friends a few years ago and the man made an incredible statement to his guests. He said he and his wife had never had a serious fight or argument in the fifty years since they were married. That was either a lot of baloney or he and his wife had a very boring relationship. Maybe both were true. To the newly married couples reading this book I must say: Don't count on having that kind of placid relationship. There *will* be times of conflict and disagreement. There *will* be periods of emotional blandness when you can generate nothing but a yawn for one another. That's life, as they say.

What will you do, then, when unexpected tornadoes blow through your home, or when the doldrums leave your sails sagging and silent? Will you pack it in and go home to Mama? Will you pout and cry and seek ways to strike back? Or will your commitment hold you steady? These questions must be addressed *now*, before Satan has an opportunity to put his noose of discouragement around your neck. Set your jaw and clench your fists. Nothing short of death must ever be permitted to come between the two of you. *Nothing!*

This determined attitude is missing from so many marital relationships today. I read of a wedding ceremony in New York a few years ago where the bride and groom each pledged "to stay with you for as long as I shall love you." I doubt if their marriage lasted even to this time. The feeling of love is simply too ephemeral to hold a relationship together for very long. It comes and goes. That's why our panel of six hundred was adamant at this point. They have lived long enough to know that a weak marital commitment will inevitably end in divorce. One writer wrote:

> Marriage is no fairy tale land of enchantment. But you can create an oasis of love in the midst of a harsh and uncaring world by grinding it out and sticking in there.

Another said:

> Perfection doesn't exist. You have to approach the first few years of marriage with a learner's permit to work out your incompatibilities. It is a continual effort.

Those views don't sound particularly romantic, do they? But they do carry the wisdom of experience. Two people are not compatible simply because they love each other and are both professing Christians. Many young couples assume that the sunshine and flowers that characterized their courtship will continue for the rest of their lives. No way, José. It is naive to expect two unique and strong-willed individuals to mesh together like a couple of machines. Even gears have multiple cogs with rough edges to be honed before they will work in concert.

That honing process usually occurs in the first year or two of marriage. The foundation for all that is to follow is laid in those critical months. What often occurs at this time is a dramatic struggle for power in the relationship. Who will lead? Who will follow? Who will determine how the money is spent? Who will get his or her way in times of disagreement? Everything is up for grabs in the beginning, and the way these early decisions are made will set the stage for the future.

Therein lies the danger. Abraham Lincoln said "A house divided against itself cannot stand." If both partners come into the relationship prepared for battle in those first two years, the foundation will begin to crumble. The apostle Paul gave us the divine perspective on human relationships—not only in marriage but in every dimension of life. He wrote, "Do nothing out of selfish ambition or vain conceit, but in humility consider others better than yourselves" (Philippians 2:3).

That one verse contains more wisdom than most marriage manuals combined. If heeded, it could virtually eliminate divorce from the catalog of human experience.

3. Communication

The third recommendation by our panel of six hundred represents another basic ingredient of good marriages. Like the other two, it begins with the letter "C" and focuses on good communication between husbands and wives. This topic has been beaten to death by writers of books on the subject of marriage, so I will hit it lightly. I would like to offer a few less overworked thoughts on marital communication, however, that might be useful to young married couples.

First, it must be understood that males and females differ yet another way not mentioned earlier. Research makes it clear that little girls are blessed with greater linguistic ability than little boys, and it remains a lifelong talent. Simply stated, she talks more than he. As an adult, she typically expresses her feelings and thoughts far better than her husband and is often irritated by his reticence. God may have given her 50,000 words per day and her husband only 25,000. He comes home from work with 24,975 used up and merely grunts his way through the evening. He may descend into Monday night football while his wife is dying to expend her remaining 25,000 words.

Erma Bombeck complained about this tendency of men to get lost in televised sports while their wives hunger for companionship. She even proposed that a new ordinance be passed which would be called "Bombeck's Law." According to it, a man who had watched 168,000 football games in a single season could be declared legally dead. All in favor say "Aye."

The complexity of the human personality guarantees exceptions to every generalization. Yet every knowledgeable marriage counselor knows that the inability or unwillingness of husbands to reveal their feelings to their wives is one of the common complaints of women. It can almost be stated as an absolute: Show me a quiet, reserved husband and I'll show you a frustrated wife. She wants to know what he's thinking and what happened at his office and how he sees the children, and especially, how he feels about her. The husband, by contrast, finds some things better left unsaid. It is a classic struggle.

"Perfection doesn't exist. You have to approach marriage with a learner's permit to work out your incompatibilities. It is a continual effort."

The paradox is that a highly emotional, verbal woman is sometimes drawn to the strong silent type. He seemed so secure and "in control" before they were married. She admired his unflappable nature and his coolness in a crisis. Then they were married and the flip side of his great strength became obvious. He wouldn't talk! She then gnashed her teeth for the next forty years because her husband *couldn't* give what she needed from him. It just wasn't in him.

Lyricist and singer Paul Simon wrote a song entitled, "I Am a Rock," which expresses the sentiment of a silent introvert. The person about whom the song is written has been wounded and has pulled within himself for protection. As you read these lyrics, imagine the special communication problems such a man and his poor wife would experience in marriage.

> A winter's day
> In a deep and dark December:
> I am alone,
> Gazing from my window
> To the streets below
> On a freshly fallen silent shroud of snow.
>
> I am a rock
> I am an island.

I've built walls,
A fortress deep and mighty,
That none may penetrate.
I have no need of friendship
Friendship causes pain.
Its laughter and its loving I disdain.

I am a rock.
I am an island.

Don't talk of love;
Well I've heard the word before;
It's sleeping in my memory.
I won't disturb the slumber of feelings that have died.
If I never loved I never would have cried.

I am a rock.
I am an island.

I have my books
And my poetry to protect me;
I am shielded in my armour,
Hiding in my room,
Safe within my womb.
I touch no one and no one touches me.

I am a rock,
I am an island.

And a rock feels no pain;
And an island never cries.[4]

Unfortunately, the wives and children of rocks and islands *do* feel pain and they do cry! But what is the solution to such communicative problems at home? As always, it involves compromise. A man has a clear responsibility to "cheer up his wife which he hath taken" (Deuteronomy 24:5). He must not claim himself "a rock" who will never allow himself to be vulnerable again. He must press himself to open his heart and share his deeper feelings with his wife. Time must be reserved for meaningful conversations. Taking walks and going out to breakfast and riding bicycles on Saturday mornings are conversation inducers that keep love alive. Communication *can* occur even in families where the husband leans inward and the wife leans outward. In these instances, I believe, the primary responsibility for compromise lies with the husband.

On the other hand, women must understand and accept the fact that some men cannot be what they want them to be. I have previously addressed this need for wives to accept reality as it is presented to them in *What Wives Wish Their Husbands Knew About Women*:

Some of the women who have read this book are married to men who will never be able to understand the feminine needs I have described. Their emotional structure makes it impossible for them to comprehend the feelings and frustrations of another—particularly those occurring in the opposite sex. These men will not read a book such as this, and would probably resent it if they did. They have never been required to "give," and have no idea how it is done. What, then, is to be the reaction of their wives? What would you do if your husband lacked the insight to be what you need him to be?

My advice is that you change that which can be altered, explain that which can be understood, teach that which can be learned, revise that which can be improved, resolve that which can be settled, and negotiate that which is open to compromise. Create the best marriage possible from the raw materials brought by two imperfect human beings with two distinctly unique personalities. But for all the rough edges which can never be smoothed and the faults which can never be eradicated, try to develop the best possible perspective and determine in your mind to accept reality exactly as it is. The first principle of mental health is to accept that which cannot be changed. You could easily go to pieces over the adverse circumstances beyond your control. You can will to hang tough, or you can yield to cowardice. Depression is often evidence of emotional surrender.

Someone wrote:

> Life can't give me joy and peace;
> it's up to me to will it.
> Life just gives me time and space;
> it's up to me to fill it.

Can you accept the fact that your husband will never be able to meet all of your needs and aspirations? Seldom does one human being satisfy every longing and hope in the breast of another. Obviously, this coin has two sides: You can't be his perfect woman, either. He is no more equipped to resolve your entire package of emotional needs than you are to become his sexual dream machine every twenty-four hours. Both partners have to settle for human foibles and faults and irritability and fatigue and occasional nighttime "headaches." A good marriage is not one where perfection reigns: It is a relationship where a healthy perspective overlooks a multitude of "unresolvables." Thank goodness my wife, Shirley, has adopted this attitude toward me!

"Can you accept the fact that your mate will never be able to meet all of your needs and aspirations?"

I am especially concerned about the mother of small children who chooses to stay at home as a full-time homemaker. If she looks to her husband as a provider of all adult conversation and the satisfier of every emotional need, their marriage can quickly run aground. He will return home from work somewhat depleted and in need of "tranquility," as we discussed earlier. Instead, he finds a woman who is continually starved for attention and support. When she sees in his eyes that he has nothing left to give, that is the beginning of sorrows. She either becomes depressed or angry (or both) and he has no idea how he can help her. I understand this feminine need and have attempted to articulate it to men. Nevertheless, a woman's total dependence on a man places too great a pressure on the marital relationship. It sometimes cracks under the strain.

What can be done, then? A woman with a normal range of emotional needs cannot simply ignore them. They scream for fulfillment. Consequently, I have long recommended that women in this situation seek to supplement what their husbands can give by cultivating meaningful female relationships. Having girl friends with whom they can talk heart to heart, study the Scriptures and share childcare techniques can be vital to mental health. Without this additional support, loneliness and low self-esteem can accumulate and begin to choke the marriage to death.

This solution of feminine company seems so obvious that one might ask why it is even worthwhile to suggest it. Unfortunately, it is not so easy to implement. A woman must often search for companionship today. We've witnessed a breakdown in relationships between women in recent years. A hundred years ago, wives and mothers did not have to seek female friendship. It was programmed into the culture. Women canned food together, washed clothes at the creek together, and cooperated in church charity work together. When babies were born, the new mother was visited by aunts, sisters, neighbors, and church women who came to help her diaper, feed, and care for the child. There was an automatic support system that surrounded women and made life easier. Its absence translates quickly into marital conflict and can lead to divorce.

To the young wives who are reading these words, I urge you *not to let this scenario happen to you*. Invest some time in your female friends—even though you are busy. Resist the temptation to pull into the walls of your home and wait for your husband to be all things to you. Stay involved as a family in a church that meets your needs and preaches the Word. Remember that you are surrounded by many other women with similar feelings. Find them. Care for them. Give to them. And in the process, your own self-esteem will rise. Then when you are content, your marriage will flourish. It sounds simplistic but that's the way we are made. We are designed to love God and to love one another. Deprivation of either function can be devastating.

oney is either
the best area of
communication in a
marriage or it is the
worst."

Money: The Great Mischief Maker

find it interesting that Jesus, who came to say so many important things and through whom the universe was made, spoke more about money than any other subject. Not only did He talk repeatedly of money, but most of His pronouncements included warnings about it. He had a dramatic encounter with a rich young ruler. He told disturbing parables about Lazarus and the rich man, and about the rich fool. He said, "For where your treasure is, there will your heart be also" (Matthew 6:21), and, "Man shall not live by bread alone, but by every word that proceedeth out of the mouth of God (Matthew 4:4). And finally, He asked a question that has echoed down through the corridors of time: "For what is a man profited, if he shall gain the whole world, and lose his own soul?" (Matthew 16:26).

Twenty centuries later, we still have to deal with that eternal question.

The intervening years have made it clear why Jesus gave such emphasis to the dangers of money. Men have lusted for it, killed for it, died for it, and gone to hell for it. Money has come between the best of friends and brought down the proud and mighty. And alas, it has torn millions of marriages limb from limb! Materialism and debt have devastated more families than perhaps any other factor, and believe me, it could destroy your marriage as well.

Men and women tend to have different value systems which precipitate arguments about money. My father, for example, was a hunter who thought nothing of using three boxes of shotgun shells in an afternoon of recreational shooting. Yet, if my mother spent an equal amount of money on a "useless" potato peeler, he considered it wasteful. Never mind that she enjoyed shopping as much as he did hunting. They simply saw things differently. On a larger scale, this divergence can produce catastrophic arguments over how to allocate limited resources.

> *"Jesus spoke more about money than any other subject."*

Curiously, those with unlimited financial resources are in no less jeopardy. One of the richest men of his time, J. Paul Getty, owned an estate that exceeded $4 billion in net worth. This is what he wrote in his autobiography as quoted in the Los Angeles Times, January 9, 1981.

> I have never been given to envy . . . save for the envy I feel toward those people who have the ability to make a marriage work and endure happily. It's an art I have never been able to master. My record: five marriages, five divorces. In short, five failures.

The article continues:

> He termed the memories of his relationship with five sons "painful." Much of his pain has been passed on with his money. His most treasured offspring, Timothy, a frail child born when Getty was fifty-three, died in 1958 at the

age of twelve of surgical complications after a sickly life spent mostly separated from his father who was forever away on business.

Other members of the Getty family also suffered from tragic circumstances. A grandson, J. Paul Getty III, was kidnapped and held for a ransom of $2.9 million. When Getty refused to pay, they held the boy for five months and eventually cut off his right ear. Getty's oldest son apparently committed suicide amid strange circumstances. Another son, Gordon Paul Getty, has been described as living a tortured existence. He was ridiculed in correspondence by his father and was the least favored son. Similar sorrow has followed other members of this unfortunate family.

Not many of us will have to worry about managing an estate the size of J. Paul Getty's. But whatever our financial status, there are monetary principles we should understand and apply if we are to protect our families. Because of the critical nature of this discussion, we are going to turn to an expert for advice. Following is an edited version of an interview I conducted with Larry Burkett on a recent Focus on the Family broadcast. Larry is president of Christian Financial Concepts, and has devoted his life to helping families live within their means. I believe the advice that follows will be especially helpful to young couples who are establishing lifelong spending habits. Now is the time to lay hold of these fundamental principles.

DOBSON: *Larry, based on your experience as a financial counselor, what is the most important advice you can give a young married couple about managing their money?*

BURKETT: Without question, the first counsel I offer is the area of credit and its potential to destroy a family. As I have often emphasized, credit is not the problem in itself, but its misuse poses a serious threat to the well-being of the home. In this context, I often tell couples to label their credit cards: "Danger—Handle with Care!"

Credit is so accessible in our society today; it can be used for every conceivable expenditure. It is very tempting for the typical family to use it to buy things they really cannot afford. By so doing, they don't avoid the inevitable payment, they only delay it, threatening their financial security in the future.

DOBSON: *Describe how that process takes place. How does a young couple manage to slide into serious credit problems?*

BURKETT: Many of the debt-ridden couples we counsel started down the road to financial ruin very early in their marriage. While the wedding bells were still ringing in their ears, they were arranging loans for cars, refrigerators, and dishwashers they really couldn't afford to own. About two years into the marriage, they were overwhelmed by their payments and decided to consolidate their debts into one loan. This maneuver helped them survive the moment, but it only forestalled the inevitable. They didn't change their spending habits and continued to use credit as a means for handling unexpected emergencies and for acquiring unnecessary items. It didn't take long before their monthly payments became too heavy again, only this time the outstanding debt was far greater. This led to feelings of hopelessness and guilt which caused them to begin arguing and blaming each other for their troubles. When they were this far down the path, bankruptcy and divorce became their likely destination.

DOBSON: *How common is that tragic scenario?*

BURKETT: I'm afraid it happens much too frequently. Studies indicate that approximately 80 percent of couples seeking divorce state that the focus of their disagreements is money.

DOBSON: *How can they avoid running their finances and their marriage into the ground?*

BURKETT: Money is either the best area of communication in a marriage or it is the worst. At the outset of their marriage, a couple must deal with questions such as: Who is going to balance the checkbook? How often will we eat out? What kind of car will we buy? How will we pay for it? How will we use credit cards?

If a husband and wife can't have meaningful discussions and reach agreements over these questions, they probably can't talk about any of the other areas so vital for a healthy relationship. That's why I recommend that every couple sit down and develop a family budget. This is not a popular idea, but I believe many people have had bad experiences with budgets because they have misunderstood the concept. There are generally three reasons why couples have failed in this area. First, some men think the budget is a weapon they can use to attack their wife's spending habits. As a result, it becomes a source of constant bickering and fighting. Second, there are those who establish an unrealistic budget that inevitably ends up in the trash. Finally, many families try to correct three years of bad spending habits in three months. They become disillusioned with the budgeting process because they couldn't succeed immediately.

> *"A budget is nothing more than a plan...it doesn't limit expenditures, it defines them."*

DOBSON: *What is the proper approach to budgeting?*

BURKETT: A budget is nothing more than a plan for spending money. It doesn't limit expenditures, it defines them. It makes this simple statement: "We have a given amount of income, and this is what we're going to do with it." If a husband and wife can agree on a basic plan and learn to appreciate each other's assets, I believe they will also begin to improve in other areas of communication as well.

DOBSON: *How do they begin to develop an outline for their spending plan?*

BURKETT: I would advise they approach their budget on an annual basis. A proper family budget is not a one-month spending plan: It is a twelve-month plan.

DOBSON: *What are the major categories they must consider, and what percentages should be allocated to them?*

BURKETT: I must be careful to point out that the percentages I provide are only guidelines. First, they should plan to set aside 10 percent of their gross income for tithing to their local church. And they can expect that the government will take 15 percent for income tax. Now let's look at the remaining amount and divide it into several categories with corresponding percentages.

Housing	36%	Insurance	5%
Property taxes		Life	
Utilities		Health	
Rent/Mortgage		Medical	
Repairs		Clothing	5%
Food	22%	Entertainment	8%
Automobile	16%	Recreation	
Car Loan		Vacations	
Fuel		Miscellaneous	8%
Repairs			

Obviously, these categories and percentages will vary according to a particular family's priorities and preferences. But this is a good place to start.

DOBSON: *Explain how these funds would actually be set aside for the intended purposes. Can you provide an example?*

BURKETT: If you are paid twice each month, I recommend you take the amount allocated for your entertainment expenses, convert it to cash and put it in an envelope marked accordingly. Then, when you go out to a restaurant, ballgame, or theater, use the money in that envelope. The key to budgeting is to stop spending for that specific category when the envelope is empty. That's the only way it will ever work.

DOBSON: *As I look at these percentages, I'm sure many people will draw the conclusion that they will need a second income in order to make it. Will sending the wife to work solve the problem?*

BURKETT: Unfortunately, if the motivation is to deal with overspending, the wife's employment will only accelerate the dilemma. She'll generate a greater income, which will give them a greater ability to borrow, and this will lead to greater debt. This contributes to a vicious cycle because she will be forced to work in order to help make payments on their loans.

DOBSON: *You are not recommending that newly married wives never seek formal employment, are you?*

BURKETT: Certainly not. I don't believe Scripture prohibits a wife from working outside the home, it just discourages it. I am merely suggesting that every young couple in the childbearing ages avoid depending on the wife's income. They must learn to live on the husband's wages. If the wife wants to work, then that income should be set aside, if possible. If they become committed to living on her income and she becomes sick or pregnant, the pressure of needing her income can eventually lead them down the credit road I described earlier. Let me reiterate. The second income is not the problem. It is indulgences and bad spending habits that create the problem.

"You can hardly become greedy or selfish when you are busily sharing what you have with others."

DOBSON: *Have you found a distinction between men and women in their attitudes concerning money?*

BURKETT: It may surprise you, Dr. Dobson, but from my experience, I've found that the big spenders in our society are not the women, as we've been led to believe. On an impulse, a woman will buy too many clothes or too much food. On the same impulse, her husband may buy a boat, car, or airplane.

DOBSON: *That's certainly a departure from conventional thinking! Isn't it true that women usually control the family's assets?*

BURKETT: While that may be true, most families in financial trouble got there because of the husband's impulsive spending. As a general rule, women are far more careful with money than men. They tend to be more security oriented and have an inherent fear of debt. For this reason, I always stress the importance of communication and balance in a couple's relationship and attitudes about money. The husband and wife should agree on their budget. It is a cooperative plan. God intended for a husband and wife to "be one flesh" (Genesis 2:24). That principle must certainly be practiced in the area of finances.

DOBSON: *Who should conduct the bookkeeping chores in a family?*

BURKETT: Assuming the couple has agreed on a spending plan, I would suggest the wife serve as bookkeeper. She is typically more disciplined and more motivated to make the budget succeed. That doesn't mean the husband yields leadership in the area of financial decisions. Remember, the more important decisions were made when the budget was established. The bookkeeper is simply allocating the expenditures that have already been predetermined.

DOBSON: *Would you agree that the ultimate responsibility for the family's finances rests with the man?*

BURKETT: Yes. As in other areas, the husband is designated in Scripture as leader in his home. He is held accountable by God for his family's well-being. I always advise that the man take a "hands-on" approach to the home finances if a problem develops.

DOBSON: *What kind of insurance is appropriate for the family struggling financially?*

BURKETT: There are two fundamental questions which must be addressed in regard to insurance. First, *How much is necessary?* Insurance should be used only to provide for the family's needs, never as a source of profit. Many couples make the mistake of using their policies as an investment tool, but these plans offer a very poor return on the investment (they may not even keep pace with inflation) and only serve the interest of the insurance company. Insurance should arrange to provide enough income to maintain the standard of living previously sustained by the principal wage earner before his death.

The second question is, *How much can you afford?* As I mentioned in our discussion of budgets, a good guideline for this expenditure is approximately

5 percent of your net income. For most families, this means that simple term insurance is the only option.

DOBSON: *If insurance is not the best investment, what is?*

BURKETT: I should preface my remarks in this area with the following axiom, "If you want my advice about investments, don't take my advice." I know what works for me, but that doesn't necessarily mean it will work for everyone else. However, I am willing to say that the average family should invest in things that have real value—items that have physical material assets. Thus, the best investment a couple can make is a home. It follows that the second best investment is rental property. If they have extra money and want to put it to use and don't mind the extra work, then they should buy a rental home, fix it up, and rent it. The value of a home will grow as fast as anything else and it has real value. Everyone needs a place to live, regardless of what happens in the economy.

Second, stay in familiar territory. Never invest in an area you don't understand. I have rarely met a doctor who made money outside of medicine. Most physicians make their money in medicine and then lose it in egg farms, ranches, and oil wells.

DOBSON: *I deeply appreciate your perspectives, Larry, because they represent scriptural absolutes that are relevant to every marriage. You've given us much to think about. If you could summarize all of your advise into a single statement what would you say?*

BURKETT: Let me conclude by repeating four simple words: *Stay out of debt.* If young couples remember nothing else I have said and retain only this concept, I can assure them that their family's financial future will not be a source of trouble.

As a final thought to these comments by Larry Burkett, I would like to emphasize the Biblical principle of tithing. I learned to give a tenth of my income to the church when I was a preschool lad. My grandmother would give me a dollar every now and then, and she always instructed me to place a dime of it in the church offering the next Sunday morning. I have tithed from that day to this. I also watched my father give of his limited resources, not only to the church but to anyone in need.

My dad was the original soft touch to those who were hungry. He was an evangelist who journeyed from place to place to hold revival meetings. Travel was expensive and we never seemed to have much more money than was absolutely necessary. One of the problems was the way churches paid their ministers in those days. Pastors received a year-round salary but evangelists were paid only when they worked. Therefore, my father's income stopped abruptly during Thanksgiving, Christmas, summer vacation, or any time he rested. Perhaps that's why we were always near the bottom of the barrel when he was at home. But that didn't stop my father from giving.

I remember Dad going off to speak in a tiny church and coming home ten days later. My mother greeted him warmly and asked how the revival had gone. He was always excited about that subject. Eventually, in moments like this she would get around to asking him about the offering. Women have a way of worrying about things like that.

"How much did they pay you?" she asked.

I can still see my father's face as he smiled and looked at the floor. "Aw . . ." he stammered. My mother stepped back and looked into his eyes.

"Oh, I get it," she said. "You gave the money away again, didn't you?"

"Myrt," he said. "The pastor there is going through a hard time. His kids are so needy. It just broke my heart. They have holes in their shoes and one of them is going to school on these cold mornings without a coat. I felt I should give the entire fifty dollars to them."

My good mother looked intently at him for a moment and then she smiled. "You know if God told you to do it, it's okay with me."

Then a few days later the inevitable happened. The Dobsons ran completely out of money. There was no reserve to tide us over. That's when my father gathered us in the bedroom for a time of prayer. I remember that day as though it were yesterday. He prayed first.

"Oh Lord, you promised that if we would be faithful with you and your people in our good times, then you would not forget us in our time of need. We have tried to be generous with what you have given us, and now we are calling on you for help."

A very impressionable ten-year-old boy named Jimmy was watching and listening very carefully that day. *What would happen?* he wondered. *Did God hear Dad's prayer?*

The next day an unexpected check for $1200 came for us in the mail. Honestly! That's the way it happened, not just this once but many times. I saw the Lord match my dad's giving stride for stride. No, God never made us wealthy, but my young faith grew by leaps and bounds. I learned that you *cannot* outgive God!

My father continued to give generously through the mid-life years and into his sixties. I used to worry about how he and Mom would fund their retirement years because they were able to save very little money. If Dad did get many dollars ahead, he'd give them away. I wondered how in the world they would live on the pittance paid to retired ministers by our denomination. (My mother now receives $80.50 per month after Dad spent forty-four years in the church. My mother's monthly allotment wouldn't get her through a single day now in the nursing home.) It is disgraceful how poorly we take care of our retired ministers and their widows.

One day my father was lying on the bed and Mom was getting dressed. She turned to look at him and he was crying.

"What's the matter?" she asked.

"The Lord just spoke to me," he replied.

"Do you want to tell me about it?" she prodded.

"He told me something about you," Dad said.

She then demanded that he tell her what the Lord had communicated to him.

My father said, "It was a strange experience. I was just lying here thinking about many things. I wasn't praying or even thinking about you when the Lord spoke to me and said, 'I'm going to take care of Myrtle.'"

Neither of them understood the message, but simply filed it away in the catalog of imponderables. But five days later my dad had a massive heart attack, and three months after that he was gone. At sixty-six years of age, this good man whose name I share went out to meet the Christ whom he had loved and served for all those years.

It has been thrilling to witness the way God has fulfilled His promise to take care of my mother. She is now suffering from end-stage Parkinson's disease and requires moment by moment care twenty-four hours a day. The cost is astronomical. Yet the small inheritance that Dad left to his wife has multiplied in the ten years since he left. It is sufficient to pay for everything she needs, including marvelous and loving care. God has been with her in every other way, too, tenderly cradling her in His secure arms. In the end, my dad never came close to outgiving God.

"God does not need your money. But you and I need to give."

May I urge you to give generously not only to your church, but also to the needy people whom God puts in your path. There is no better way to keep material things and money in proper perspective. You can hardly become selfish or greedy when you are busily sharing what you have with others. You see, God does not need your money. He could fund his ministries from an annual beef auction alone (He owns the cattle on a thousand hills). But you and I *need* to give! Those who comprehend and respond to this Biblical principle will find that He is faithful to "open the windows of heaven, and pour you out a blessing, that there shall not be room enough to receive it" (Malachi 3:10). And don't forget the greatest blessing of all: The curly headed, impressionable children around your feet will be watching and will someday pass the good news on to *their* kids! That may be your greatest legacy on this earth.

The surge of passion derives from his touch and his tenderness toward her."

A Few Basic Facts About Sex

t is impossible to tell young men and women all they need to know about marital sex in so brief a context, so I will not even attempt it. Rather, I strongly suggest that engaged or newlywed couples obtain a set of tapes produced by Dr. Ed Wheat, entitled "Before the Wedding Night." These recordings are excellent and can be obtained in local Christian bookstores. They are designed to be listened to together and then used as a basis for discussion and study. Though the title indicates otherwise, the tapes are also useful for those who are already married.

We will restrict our focus at this point, then, to two primary—yet basic—concepts. A great amount of anxiety and conflict can be eliminated just by grasping these fundamental understandings:

1. *Don't be surprised if sexual intercourse is less intense than anticipated on the honeymoon.* For those who have saved themselves for that first night, their level of expectation may exceed reality by a wide margin. For those who have had intercourse before, disappointment is also possible. Because sexual desire is sometimes greater when it reaches for forbidden fruit than when it is obligatory, stolen moments in the past may have surpassed the marital experience in pleasure and intensity.

Every couple is different, of course, and there are no generalizations that apply to everyone. Nevertheless, it is common for sexual problems (or sexual coolness, at least) to occur in early married life. For one thing, the transformation from "Thou shalt not" to "Thou shalt, regularly and with great passion" is not so easily made by some people. It takes time for one mindset to give way to another. Second, sexual intercourse in human beings is a highly complex mental process. Copulation for animals is simply a matter of hormones and opportunity. For people, however, the frame of mind, the setting, the sense of security, the aromas, the visualizations, the partner's attitude and one's own modesty all come into play. That's why you shouldn't be surprised or disappointed if everything fails to "click" on the first night . . . or even the first month.

"Sex can still be exciting and new after 30 or 40 years of marriage, because individuals are still learning how to please one another."

Erma Bombeck has gone so far as to recommend separate honeymoons for husbands and wives. That's crazy, of course, but the first week or two of married life *can* produce some hilarious experiences. The best honeymoon story I've heard came from some friends close to Shirley and me. After a fancy wedding they drove to a local hotel and checked into the bridal suite. The new husband glided into the bathroom to freshen up and his wife awaited his grand entrance. During that interlude, she noticed that a large bottle of champagne had been delivered to their room, compliments of the hotel. The bride had never tasted an alcoholic beverage before, but she did recall that her doctor recommended a small quantity of wine to settle her honeymoon jitters. *Why not?* she thought. She poured herself a glass of bubbly and found she liked it quite well. She quickly poured and drank another glass and continued guzzling until the bottle was almost empty. That's when it hit her. The groom stepped out of the bathroom expectantly and found his bleary-eyed bride clutching a champagne bottle and grinning from ear to ear. She was stone-cold drunk. He smelled like after-shave lotion and she smelled like a skid-row bum. The young wife then became deathly ill and "tossed her cookies"—including the awful wedding cake—for several hours. That cooled down the groom considerably. He sat up with her through the night and helped her get dressed the next morning. They had to catch an early plane to Hawaii although the bride was in poor condition to travel. She was still drunk and had to be led, weaving and groaning, to the airport. She did not regain her equilibrium for two more days. By then, the groom had forgotten what he came for. This delightful couple has now been married for twenty-two years and neither has been drunk since. But they will tell you, if you ask, that honeymoons are made for trouble!

If your honeymoon is also a tragicomedy, take heart. Things will get better. You *will* learn. Amazingly, sex can still be exciting and new after thirty or forty years of marriage because individuals are continuing to learn how to please themselves and one another. The critical thing is not to panic if initial disappointments are encountered. Fears and failures, if experienced early in the relationship, can cause the sexual response to shut down in order to prevent any further emotional pain. That need not happen if one's level of expectations can be lowered going into marriage. You have a lifetime to enjoy one another. But don't demand too much too soon . . . and stay away from pink champagne.

2. Men and women differ significantly in their sexual appetites, and those differences should be comprehended by both the husband and wife. For a man, intercourse is much more physiological than it is for a woman. This means that he is more easily stimulated visually and typically becomes excited more quickly than she. Within moments, the idea of sexual relations can enter his mind, and four or five minutes later the act might be finished and he is asleep again. She lies awake resenting him and regretting the brief episode. One woman even told me that her sex life with her husband reminded her of an old silent movie . . . not a word was exchanged between them. The movie might well be titled, "Romancing the Stone."

A husband and wife *must* understand that she doesn't function that way. First, the way she feels about her husband sexually is a byproduct of their romantic relationship at that time. If she feels close to him . . . loved by him . . . protected by him . . . then she is more likely to desire him physically. Merely seeing his body does not do that much for her. Yes, she is interested in how he looks, but the surge of passion comes not from a stolen glance but from the quality of their interaction. It derives from his touch and his tenderness toward her.

> *"The way a woman feels about her husband sexually is a by-product of their romantic relationship at the time."*

There has been ample evidence of this difference between the sexes, both scientific and pragmatic. Ann Landers was contacted a few years ago, for example, by a female reader who posed this challenge:

Dear Ann Landers,

Often I have been tempted to write to you and express another viewpoint when letters appeared that I did not agree with. The motivation was never strong enough—until now.

I cannot rest until I respond to the man who wanted a penis implant. He said his anxiety over not being able to complete the sex act with the woman he loves was driving him crazy because he knew she must feel deprived and unfulfilled.

For him I have one word, Hogwash. It's his ego talking. That man is totally ignorant of the workings of the female mind and heart. If you were to ask 100 women how they feel about sexual intercourse, 98 would say, "Just hold me close and be tender. Forget about the act."

If you don't believe it, why not take a poll? Your readership is phenomenal and people tell you things they would never tell anyone else. How about it, Ann? Will you ask them?

Longtime Faithful in Oregon

Ann replied:

Dear Faithful:

You're on! I am asking the women in my reading audience to send a postcard or letter (P.O. Box 11995, Chicago, Ill. 60611) with a reply to the question: Would you be content to be held close and treated tenderly and forget about "the act?" Reply YES or NO and please add one line. "I am over (or under) 40 years of age." No signature is necessary.

A few months later, Ann published this follow-up comment in her column.

Well dear readers, to date I have received more than 90,000 responses and they are still pouring in. The mail room looks like a disaster area. We have put on extra help. The employees are working double shifts and weekends, yet the mailbags seem to multiply like rabbits. Since I have been writing this column the only time the response was heavier was when I asked my readers to clip the column, sign it and send it to President Reagan. That column was about nuclear war. This sex survey beats the meat loaf recipe, the lemon pie and the poll asking parents, "If you had it to do over again, would you have children?" (Seventy percent said no.)

Mercifully, the vast majority of respondents sent postcards, but a surprising number of women felt compelled to write letters. Some went on for three and four pages, explaining why they felt as they did.

I believe the intense interest in this poll makes a statement about what goes on behind closed doors in the bedrooms of the world. Keep in mind my column appears in Canada, Europe, Tokyo, Hong Kong, Bangkok, Mexico City and a variety of other places around the world. And the mail came from everywhere. It also says something about communication and fulfillment (or the lack of it) among great numbers of couples who are having sexual relations—both married and unmarried.

Was I surprised at the outcome of the poll? Yes—but not very. I could have guessed the way it would go. But I never dreamed that more than 90,000 women would be moved to express themselves on this highly intimate subject. Nor would I have predicted the percentages or the passion with which so many women described their sex lives.

The greatest revelation to me at least, is what the poll says about men as lovers. Clearly, there is trouble in paradise.

Tomorrow I will print the results as well as excerpts from letters. That column is sure to be a topic of conversation in bars, drawing rooms, beauty shops and sociology classes for a long time to come.

The next day she released the results of the poll. These were her findings:

More than 90,000 women cast their ballots. Seventy-two percent said yes they would be content to be held close and treated tenderly and forget about the act. Of those 72 percent who said yes, 40 percent were under 40 years old. That was the most surprising aspect of the survey.

Many women who voted no said they needed the sexual climax to relieve physical tension. Almost as many said they wanted the ultimate in gratification—that anything less would make them feel exploited and used.

A 32 year old from Atlanta put it this way. He insists on getting his satisfaction so why shouldn't I have mine?

Columbus, Ohio. I am under 40 and would be delighted to settle for tender words and warm caresses. The rest of it is a bore and can be exhausting. I am sure the sex act was designed strictly for the pleasure of males.

Anchorage, Alaska. I am under 40, 26 to be exact. I want three children, so obviously I need more than conversation. After I have my family, I would happily settle for separate rooms. Sex doesn't do a thing for me.

Westport, Connecticut. I vote yes. My husband is a diabetic and hasn't been able to perform for 10 years. I would have voted yes 20 years ago. He never bothered to satisfy me when he had his health. His illness was a blessing.

Kansas City. I am 55 and vote yes. The best part is the cuddling and caressing and the tender words that come with caring. My first husband used to rape me about five times a week. If a stranger had treated me like that I would have had him arrested.

Chicago. I don't want either his tender words or the act. My husband became impotent from alcoholism 10 years ago. The only word I'd like from him is "goodbye," but the bum won't leave.

Helena, Montana. No. I am 32. To say that touching and tender words are sufficient is like settling for the smell of fresh baked bread and ignoring the nourishment it provides. Such people must be crazy.

Texarkana. Yes. Without the tender embrace the act is animalistic. For years I hated sex and felt used. I was relieved when my husband died. My present mate is on heart pills that have made him impotent. It's like heaven to be held and cuddled.

Washington, D. C. Yes, yes a million times yes. I would love to be spoken to tenderly. It would be enough. My boyfriend never says a word. If I say anything he says, "Be quiet. You're spoiling things."

Eureka. I am 62 and voting no. If my old man was over the hill I would settle for high-school necking, but as long as he's able to shake the walls and wake up the neighbors downstairs, I want to get in on the action. And I'll take an encore anytime I can get it.[5]

Would you have believed that 72 percent of the women who responded care only about loving closeness and tenderness? I would, after having surveyed more than 10,000 women in polls of my own. It boils down to this: Women often give sex to get intimacy and men give intimacy to get sex. Believe me, that difference has enormous implications. A man can enjoy a quick romp in bed, even if he and his wife have argued and bickered all evening. In some ways it is even more exciting for him to "conquer" this woman who has engaged him in verbal battle. For her, sex under those circumstances makes her feel "used" by her husband . . . almost like a prostitute. This difference in orientation has set off a million fiery-tempered confrontations between husbands and wives who didn't really understand why the other was frustrated. Because women are more romantically inclined, the man who wants an exciting sexual relationship with his wife should focus on the *other* 23½ hours in the day. He should compliment her, bring her flowers and tell her that he cares. These are the ingredients of genuine passion. Author Kevin Leman has gone a step further. He said the greatest of all aphrodisiacs is for a man to take out the garbage for his wife. I agree.

> *"You have a lifetime to enjoy one another. Don't demand too much too soon."*

To make the most of the physical dimension of marriage, a man must pursue his wife's *mind* as well as her body. They cannot be separated. Turning the coin over, the woman should make herself as attractive to her husband as possible. Forget the curlers, cold cream, and flannel pajamas. He is a creature of vision and she is a lover of touch. By a little unselfish forethought, each can learn to excite the other. The differences between them is what makes the game interesting.

In conclusion, sex is at its best when both partners are "lost" in the excitement of unselfconscious passion. That is most likely to occur when each person feels respected by the other and when the act of intercourse is merely a vehicle for the expression of love. That's the way it was intended to be. In the absence of that affection, the momentary thrill of copulation gives way to disgust or boredom. It becomes a performance to be evaluated critically. Ask the lush in the singles bar who sleeps with a different person every night. He or she will tell you there is no real satisfaction in mating with a stranger. An alley cat can do that. The real challenge is in achieving monogamous, loving, caring, romantic, mutually satisfying sexual union. Once you find the formula for that experience, it can be repeated for a lifetime.

Settle for nothing less . . . but don't expect to find it on your honeymoon.

*T*he restrictions
and commandments of
Scripture were designed
to protect us from evil."

The Marriage Killers

few years ago, Shirley and I took a vacation with our family and ended the trip in Washington, D.C. I had heard there was to be a special briefing on the family at the White House that day and I decided at the last minute to attend. Because I was not on the guest list it took me about ten minutes longer to get through White House security, and I slipped into the briefing room just before the first speaker was announced. I sat down behind my good friend, Lalani Watt, wife of then Secretary of the Interior, James Watt.

Lalani greeted me and then said, "I don't think they've done you right."

I said, "Why not? What do you mean?"

She said, "They didn't give you enough time."

"Time?" I replied, "Time for what?"

"Why, time to speak," she said. "Didn't you know you're on the program today?"

At that moment a White House aide tapped me on the shoulder and asked if he could usher me to the platform. Apparently, members of the staff who planned the briefing had known that I was likely to be there but had failed to tell me they were expecting me to speak! It was quite a shock to find myself looking at two hundred expectant professionals who awaited my words of wisdom. I looked down and noticed that I had on brown socks and a blue suit. It had been a long vacation and I wore the only clean thing left in my suitcase.

Who knows, and who cares, what I said to those men and women that day. Whether I captured their attention is doubtful, but the White House Staff certainly grabbed mine! I went from half asleep to supercharged in a period of four seconds. Fortunately for the audience, there were other speakers on the program that day, and one of them said some things I will never forget.

His name was Dr. Armand Nicholi, a psychiatrist at Harvard University Medical School and Massachusetts General Hospital. He spoke on the subject of parenting, especially as it relates to the mental health of children. I wish every mother and father could have heard his remarks as he quoted the latest research on the consequences of divorce and family disintegration.

According to Dr. Nicholi, it is now known that emotional development in children is directly related to the presence of a warm, nurturing, sustained, and continuous interaction with *both* parents. Anything that interferes with the vital relationship with either parent can have lasting consequences for the child. One landmark study revealed that 90 percent of the children from divorced homes suffered from an acute sense of shock when the separation occurred, including profound grieving and irrational fears. Fifty percent reported feeling rejected and abandoned, and indeed, half the fathers never came to see their children three years after the divorce. One-third of the boys and girls feared abandonment by the remaining parent with an intensity that researchers described as "overwhelming." Most significantly, 37 percent of the children were even more unhappy and dissatisfied five years after the divorce than they had been at eighteen months. In other words, *time did not heal their wounds.*

In summary, Dr. Nicholi said divorce brings such intense loneliness to children that its pain is difficult to describe or even contemplate.

"Divorce brings such loneliness to children that its pain is difficult to describe or even contemplate...time does not heal their wounds."

We all know that divorce has become the fashionable way to deal with marital conflict in the past three decades. Books such as *Creative Divorce* have described it as the start of a brand new life that was in the "best interest" of the entire family. But that is patently untrue. Divorce is devastating, not just for the children but for their hurt and angry parents, too. Women pay a particularly high price, even when they are the ones who opted out of the relationship.

Let me explain. There have always been irresponsible men who were unfaithful to their wives or abandoned their families. That is still going on and accounts for millions of broken homes today. But in my lifetime, marriages have begun to disintegrate for another reason. Women, encouraged by new freedoms and financial security, have shown a greater willingness to pull the plug. I have worked with many frustrated wives who seemed determined to obtain a divorce, not because their husbands were unfaithful or irresponsible, but because romantic love was missing from the relationship. These women expressed great anger and deep resentment toward husbands who were either unwilling or unable to meet their wives' basic emotional needs.

I would not minimize the distressing "soul hunger" that women so frequently describe, but I will say this: Divorce is not the answer to it! Those who seek that "solution" often jump from the frying pan into the fire!

That is the point of the book entitled *Marriage: Grounds for Divorce*, written by Monte Vanton. The author was divorced by his wife and seemed quite bitter about the experience. Yet his analysis of marital breakup is insightful and provocative. Following are excerpts that convey his thesis. See if you agree with his perspective, keeping in mind that Vanton did not write from a Christian viewpoint.

> The end of a marriage is like a little death, but to some married women, freedom looks like life after death. Young again, no one to tell her what to do, no more demands, criticisms. No more dinners to cook—no slavery! And, just outside, bright lights, gay conversation, lighthearted friends, flirtations and adventures. Palm Springs, Vegas, here I come!

> A free spirit again! Oh, what a wonderful world it will be. No more arguments, complaints, no more asking for money. I'll have my own for evermore! Do you know a good attorney?

> For the first few months, things do seem to improve. The cessation of hostilities is pleasant. Since the wife for years experienced an emotional tug-of-war in her mixed-up role as woman, wife and leader, the sudden severance brings temporary relief. But only temporary.

> What is the chief preoccupation of our newly arrived divorcée? Career, children, home, travel, art, politics, friends. No, it's men! Where do these men come from? What are they like? What do they want? What have they been doing?

Hope is wonderful, but fantasy can be catastrophic! Many women, divorced or married and contemplating divorce, are sure that somewhere outside there is a man who will have all the virtues of her husband and none of his vices. From this starting point, divorcées start the great search.

It is obvious that the husband must have had some good points—hence the original marriage. The fact the husband is a known quantity and the new man an unknown hazard, places him far ahead of the stranger. There is a good chance that another man may have similar or even more pronounced defects, since he lives in the same culture with the same standards and values. Further, how can our gal judge clearly? How does she know she won't repeat the same mistake?

Her problem is further compounded. In her first marriage, she was trusting and open—now she is certain to be more cynical and guarded.

In the selection of a new mate, she must take into consideration the fact he may not want someone else's youngsters—can she be sure he will be good to them? And if indeed the new man is kind, there is always the chance the children may imperil their marital bliss by serving as a constant reminder they are not his own.

Where does this dream man come from?

Divorcées are usually between the ages of twenty-eight and thirty-nine at starting point.

There are basically two categories of men in this age group, the divorced and the never married. Our gal tries to avoid the latter. He spells trouble—a mother or a mother's memory lurking somewhere in the background. He's probably set in his ways, old-womanish or a happy seducer. Or—he's just not moved by women. In any event, the outlook is far from kosher. That leaves the man who has been married. Why did his wife divorce him? He might be as poor a bet as one's ex-husband.

Well, the field is narrowed to ages thirty-five to forty. We'll take a chance that he has been married before. What should he look like? Well, as long as we're changing husbands, he should be good-looking. Tall? Sure! Virile? Of course! Didn't we say that one of the troubles with our husbands was their indifference to sex? Actually, he should be a little like Cary Grant, have a nice speaking voice, be a good conversationalist, popular with men, romantic, decisive, tender, poetic, passionate, and above all, understanding. And he shouldn't have a mother!

He should have unlimited money and an interesting career—not a blouse manufacturer, or an auctioneer—a writer perhaps, or a lecturer, diplomat, or maybe just a millionaire. "After all, I want my kids to have the best. Why make a change if I don't improve myself? And he should love me completely and never make demands on me or be possessive. Nor should he ever criticize my housekeeping. He should never be tired, preoccupied or make an issue about money. He should take me away weekends, and out to a nice restaurant on Sunday morning for breakfast. We would travel a lot, and he should always be interested, completely interested in me!"

There are several million women, married, single and divorced looking for this hero—and he hasn't been found yet. But the girls keep hoping and looking.

The only place he exists is in a hit record, on a TV or movie screen or in one's imagination.

Forget the dreams of money, charm, career, manliness and decisiveness—and the chances of landing a skinny, broke, thin-haired, petulant, hollow-chested male are great.

The male has suddenly become King! All the gals are after him. His stock has leaped upwards; he never had it so good, and he's going to keep it coming. Marriage? That would end it all! He doesn't have to do anything. He's a male.

The chance of landing the ideal man is one in a million. Have you ever considered, ladies, the attitude of the eligible male? Marriage is the last thing he wants! Suddenly, the world has become his oyster and, after years of marriage, monotony and misery, his ego crushed, his manhood challenged, he's free and it's a man's world. Daily he is reminded by suppliant females that he's a hero! Why should he give that up! Besides, he's wily and experienced; he has learned the hard way.

He isn't going to be trapped by promises of home-cooked meals, a seductive figure and the prospect of heady nights beside the TV. Like an old salmon in a well-fished stream, he can smell the hook a mile away.

"Don't permit the possibility of divorce to enter your thinking. Even in moments of great conflict and discouragement, divorce is no solution."

The ex-husband knows this moment of triumph all too quickly comes to an end once he says: "I do." He knows the law is slanted toward the female, and he knows there are thousands of attorneys all ready to aid the "little woman" once she decides to shed her husband and enjoy his substance. Why should he fall for that?

What does he want? It's really very simple. An occasional date, proper respect and then to bed—no strings. And when he takes you to bed he feels he's doing you a service! Oh, he's a hard man. Of course you don't have to go to bed with him. If he really digs you, he might wait three, maybe four dates, and then, no bed and he's gone. So you do go to bed; after all, you're human and he's likeable. From the moment of conquest he starts a rear guard action. Demonstrations of affection from you are regarded as warning signals, and he starts to pull away.

And so, life passes pleasantly for our male. He has his work, friends, apartment, vacations, ball games, and of course, his women, all loving, never demanding, never possessive, and all telling him what a wonderful lover he is. And then there are so many women out there he hasn't yet met. What an exciting prospect!

But you say, "He's a fool. He doesn't know what he's missing—a home, a family, a loving wife, permanence, security, building something together." But, he does know what he's missing. He had a home—worked hard to get it. His wife got that! He had a family, and loved his kids. His wife got those too. Permanence he never had—his wife's attorney shattered his hearth. Security— here today, gone tomorrow. The things he built with his wife, his wife and her attorney shared between them. Ms. Divorcée, you have paved the way for another woman's failure to catch a man, and another woman has facilitated your failure.

Men complain about unfair divorce laws, the flimsy excuses women use to obtain divorces, the distribution of the hard-worked-for assets, the alimony, and they say, it's all one-sided. Your wife picks up the tab with your money when she takes her boyfriend out to dinner. And then some other husband pays the tab when his ex-wife takes you out. Things balance out.

To meet this shift in social standards and provide a place where lonely women might meet men, some bright girls started a club which has enjoyed some success. It's called "Parents Without Spouses." Because there are so few places where divorcées can meet men, "Parents Without Spouses" sponsors dances.

Divorcées eagerly anticipate these events, dress carefully, and sally forth to the big adventure.

I have never seen the Chicago stock yards—but I have seen these dances! They are frightening and desperate like a slave auction! The allure of the female fades as hordes of them smile, gesture, pose and parade. Strong men blanch at the prospect.

The market is reversed and the man is desperately hunted, but he doesn't want to be chased—he wants to do the chasing! There is something frightening about being chased by a female and being chased by a thousand is positively terrifying.

There was once a movie called *The Gay Divorcée*. A charming, beautiful, divorced woman was depicted floating from one deliriously exciting adventure to another. Admired, flattered by an army of doting males, envied by her poor married sisters, she became a sort of symbol for American womanhood. The longed for, hoped for state of freedom. But this was a movie, it was fiction and fantasy, yet our Cinderella mentality still continues.

Most divorcées sit at home at night and when the phone rings it is a reprieve. Parents are really no help, they only remind you you're getting older and lonelier.

Married friends feel a little uncomfortable with you, on guard lest you think them patronizing. They eventually disappear. You got the kids, and you got the responsibilities. Double. Other divorced women speak your language but you hate it! On vacations word gets around that you're a divorcée and immediately ideas are formed about you. Married women think you are loose and dangerous—and cluck protectively around their husbands. Men are amazed if you don't go to bed with them on the first date. You've lost your citizenship, your status! You have freedom—you stay home. Night after night as the hours tick away, loneliness is increased by fear. Self-confidence begins to ooze away, and in that quiet apartment a ghost enters and takes you by the hand. You wonder if you've forgotten how to talk, how to be witty. You begin to feel unattractive, despised.

Given enough time in that room, and whatever ugly mental self-image you have concealed all these years, gradually emerges and takes over. So you rush to the telephone and start calling. Striving to keep a cheerful note in your voice, and having nothing new to say, you ask, "What's new?" When women friends' numbers give out, you apprehensively dial some men friends, hoping they are not entertaining other females. Trying to sound casual, and praying your anxiety won't show, you chattily ask: "What's new? I haven't heard from you for some time. Been out of town? Yes, we must get together sometime." Maybe I should have gone to bed with him last time—he sounded a little cold.

A date brings relief, but the loneliness of yesterday is the herald of tomorrow's fears.

Millions of women know this. Yet today there are thousands of women about to tell their husbands they have decided to get a divorce, and tomorrow there will be thousands more.

When birth control became generally accepted, intelligent women quickly availed themselves of this simple technique. The need warranted the use. Is there not as great a need for divorce control? Why is one precaution so important, the other non-existent?[6]

Whether or not you agree with Vanton's distressing analysis (I think he's dead right about female disillusionment but he understates seriously the pain experienced by men) my advice to young couples stands unchallenged: Don't permit the *possibility* of divorce to enter your thinking. Even in moments of great conflict and discouragement, divorce is no solution. It merely substitutes a new set of miseries for the ones left behind. Guard your relationship against erosion as though you were defending your very lives. Yes, you *can* make it together. Not only can you survive, but you can keep your love alive if you give it priority in your system of values.

It is true, of course, that the society in which we live actively mitigates against marital stability. There are dangers on all sides, and we must defend ourselves with all our energies. In fact, I think it would be healthy at this point to name the great marriage killers. Any one of the following evils can rip your relationship to shreds if given a place in your lives. We have touched on some of these items, but perhaps it would be helpful to list them all and provide a comment for a few:

1. *Overcommitment and physical exhaustion.* Beware of this danger. It is especially insidious for young couples who are trying to get started in a profession or in school. Do *not* try to go to college, work full-time, have a baby, manage a toddler, fix up a house and start a business at the same time. It sounds ridiculous, but many young couples do just that and are then surprised when their marriage falls apart. Why wouldn't it? The only time they see each other is when they are worn out! It is especially dangerous to have the husband vastly overcommitted and the wife staying home with a preschooler. Her profound loneliness builds discontent and depression, and we all know where that leads. You *must* reserve time for one another if you want to keep your love alive.

2. *Excessive credit and conflict over how money will be spent.* We've said it before: Pay *cash* for consumable items or don't buy. Don't spend more for a house

or car than you can afford, leaving too few resources for dating, short trips, baby-sitters, etc. Allocate your funds with the wisdom of Solomon.

3. *Selfishness.* There are two kinds of people in the world, the givers and the takers. A marriage between two givers can be a beautiful thing. Friction is the order of the day, however, for a giver and a taker. But two takers can claw each other to pieces within a period of six weeks. In short, selfishness will devastate a marriage every time.

4. *Interference from in-laws.* If either the husband or wife have not been fully emancipated from the parents, it is best not to live near them. Autonomy is difficult for some mothers (and fathers) to grant, and close proximity is built for trouble.

5. *Unrealistic expectations.* Some couples come into marriage anticipating rose-covered cottages, walks down primrose lanes and uninterrupted joy. Counselor Jean Lush believes, and I agree, that this romantic illusion is particularly characteristic of American women who expect more from their husbands than they are capable of delivering. The consequent disappointment is an emotional trap. Bring your expectations in line with reality.

6. *Space invaders.* This killer will be difficult to describe or understand in such a brief context, but I'll try. By space invaders, I am *not* referring to aliens from Mars. Rather, my concern is for those who violate the breathing room needed by their partners, quickly suffocating them and destroying the attraction between them. Jealousy is one way this phenomenon manifests itself. Another is low self-esteem which leads the insecure spouse to trample the territory of the other. Love *must* be free and it must be confident. (If more information is needed, read my earlier book, *Love Must Be Tough.*)

7. *Alcohol or substance abuse.* These are killers, not only of marriages but of people. Avoid them like the plague.

8. *Pornography, gambling, and other addictions.* It should be obvious to everyone that the human personality is flawed. It has a tendency to get hooked on destructive behaviors, especially early in life. During an introductory stage, people think they can play with enticements such as pornography or gambling and not get hurt. Indeed, many do walk away unaffected. For some, however, there is a weakness and a vulnerability that is unknown until too late. Then they become addicted to something that tears at the fabric of the family. This warning may seem foolish and even prudish to my readers, but I've made a twenty-year study of those who wreck their lives. Their problems often begin in experimentation with a known evil and ultimately ends in death . . . or the death of a marriage.

Personally, I've not permitted myself to even taste certain vices, knowing that I can never become addicted to something if it is not granted a toehold in my life. For example, Shirley and I have gone to Las Vegas without ever putting a nickel in a slot machine, even though two rolls of coins were provided with hotel reservations. I refused to use them for the same reason the hotel manager gave them to me. He knew if he could open the door to insignificant gambling I might walk through it. But I wouldn't play his game. Likewise, Shirley and I are teetotalers when it comes to alcohol. I know many people enjoy wine with their meals—and that is entirely their business. But neither we nor our children will ever have a problem with alcohol if we take an absolutist position in reference to it. Obviously, I am not in a position to recommend that everyone do as we have done, but there would be fewer divorces if others did.

As a member of the Attorney General's Commission on Pornography, I listened to testimony by those who thought they could jazz up their sex lives with obscene materials. They discovered that the stuff they were watching quickly began to seem tame and even boring. That led them to seek racier, more explicit depictions. And then they journeyed unexpectedly down the road toward harder and more offensive materials. For some, not all, it became an obsession that filled their world with perversion and sickness. They lusted after sex with animals, molestation of children, urinating and defecation, sado-masochism, mutilation of the genitals, and incest. And how did it happen? The door was quietly opened and a monster came charging out. My point is this: The restrictions and commandments of Scriptures were designed to protect us from evil. Though it is difficult to believe when we are young, "The wages of sin is death" (Romans 6:23). If we keep our lives clean and do not permit ourselves to toy with evil, the addictions which have ravaged humanity can never touch us. It's a very old-fashioned idea. I still believe in it.

9. *Sexual frustration, loneliness, low self-esteem, and the greener grass of infidelity.* A deadly combination!

10. *Business failure.* It does bad things to men, especially. Their agitation over financial reverses sometimes sublimates to anger within the family.

11. *Business success.* It is almost as risky to succeed wildly as it is to fail miserably in business. Solomon wrote, "Give me neither poverty nor riches, but give me only my daily bread" (Proverbs 30:8). Edward Fitzgerald said it another way: "One of the saddest pages kept by the recording angel is the record of souls that have been damned by success." It's true. Those who profit handsomely sometimes become drunk with power and the lust for *more!* Wives and children are forgotten in the process.

12. *Getting married too young.* Girls who marry between fourteen and seventeen years of age are more than twice as likely to divorce as those who marry at eighteen or nineteen years of age. Those who marry at eighteen or nineteen are 1.5 times as likely to divorce as those who marry in their twenties. The pressures of adolescence and the stresses of early married life do not mix well. Finish the first before taking on the second.

"Guard your relationship against erosion as though you were defending your very lives."

These are the bloody marriage killers I've seen most often. But in truth, the list is virtually limitless. All that is needed to grow the most vigorous weeds is a small crack in your sidewalk. If you are going to beat the odds and maintain an intimate, long-term marriage, you must take the task seriously. The natural order of things will carry you away from one another, not bring you together.

Let me put it another way. Not far from where I was born, the mighty Mississippi winds its way through the countryside. It is a beautiful river but has a will of its own. Approximately seventy miles from Baton Rouge, Louisiana, the government is fighting a tremendous battle to keep this powerful river from changing its course to a shorter and steeper descent to the Gulf of Mexico. If the Mississippi has its way, the results will be catastrophic for cities and farms on the downward side. The entire topography of southern Louisiana would change. The port cities of New Orleans and Baton Rouge would lose their waterfront and their way of life. A town called Morgan City would be flooded into oblivion. Engineers estimate that billions of dollars of property would be destroyed if this battle is lost, and the outcome is still in doubt.

In some ways, the battle to save the family is like that. Without considerable effort and expenditure of resources, the banks will overflow and the landscape will be ruined. That's the world in which we live. As we said in the first chapter, only one or two marriages in ten will generate the intimacy so desperately sought.

Let me repeat the questions asked earlier: How will you beat the odds? How will you build a solid relationship that will last until death takes you across the great divide? How will you include yourselves among that dwindling number of older couples who have garnered a lifetime of happy memories and experiences? Even after fifty or sixty years, they still look to one another for encouragement and understanding. Their children have grown up in a stable and loving environment and have no ugly scars or bitter memories to erase. Their grandchildren need not be told, delicately, why "Nana and Papa don't live together any more." Only love prevails. That is the way God intended it to be, and it is still possible for you to achieve. But there is no time to lose. Reinforce the river banks. Brace up the bulwarks. Bring in the dredges and deepen the bed. Keep the powerful currents in their proper channels. Only that measure of determination will preserve the love with which you began, and there is very little in life that competes with that priority. If you don't agree, read this book again. You missed something vital.